Recipes from the World of H.P. Lovecraft

Thunder Bay Press
An imprint of Printers Row Publishing Group
9717 Pacific Heights Blvd, San Diego, CA 92121
www.thunderbaybooks.com • mail@thunderbaybooks.com

Printers Row Publishing Group is a division of Readerlink Distribution Services, LLC.
Thunder Bay Press is a registered trademark of Readerlink Distribution Services, LLC.

Correspondence regarding the content of this book should be sent to Thunder Bay Press, Editorial Department, at the above address. Author and rights inquiries should be addressed to Pyramid, an imprint of Octopus Publishing Group Ltd., Carmelite House, 50 Victoria Embankment, London, EC4Y 0DZ, www.octopusbooks.co.uk

Thunder Bay Press
Publisher: Peter Norton • Associate Publisher: Ana Parker
Editor: Dan Mansfield

Produced by Pyramid
Publisher: Lucy Pessell
Senior Editor: Hannah Coughlin • Designer: Isobel Platt
Assistant Editor: Samina Rahman
Project Editor: Tara O'Sullivan
Recipe Development: Jane Birch
Production Controllers: Lucy Carter and Nic Jones

Library of Congress Control Number: 2022949042

ISBN: 978-1-6672-0232-7

Printed in China

27 26 25 24 23 1 2 3 4 5

Recipes from the World of H. P. Lovecraft

recipes inspired by cosmic horror

Olivia Luna Eldritch

THUNDER BAY
P·R·E·S·S

San Diego, California

Contents

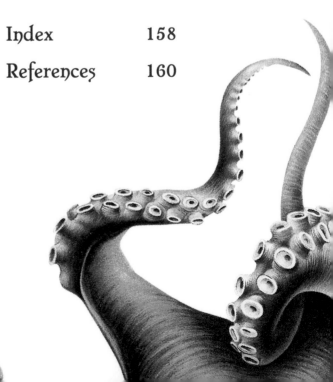

Introduction

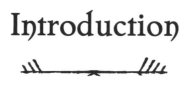

"Searchers after horror haunt strange, far places. For them are the catacombs of Ptolemais, and the carven mausolea of the nightmare countries. They climb to the moonlit towers of ruined Rhine castles, and falter down black cobwebbed steps beneath the scattered stones of forgotten cities in Asia. The haunted wood and the desolate mountain are their shrines, and they linger around the sinister monoliths on uninhabited islands. But the true epicure in the terrible, to whom a new thrill of unutterable ghastliness is the chief end and justification of existence, esteems most of all the ancient, lonely farmhouses of backwoods New England; for there the dark elements of strength, solitude, grotesqueness and ignorance combine to form the perfection of the hideous."

—"The Picture in the House"

Although he never achieved great success in his own lifetime, H. P. Lovecraft has since become renowned as one of the most significant writers of horror of the twentieth century, leaving behind him an enormous legacy that inspired countless other writers and spawned an entire mythos of gods, monsters, and cosmic entities. From the iconic tentacled Cthulhu to the sinister medical student Herbert West, Lovecraft's creations have taken on a life of their own—and in this book, we will be celebrating and exploring some of his most terrifying works. The best way to share stories is, of course, over a meal, and for that reason, we have gathered a selection

of delectable delights inspired by the weird and wonderful mind of this most remarkable writer.

Howard Phillips Lovecraft was born on August 20, 1890, in Providence, Rhode Island. He discovered the work of Edgar Allan Poe as a young boy, and quickly developed a love for gothic fiction, along with a keen interest in science, especially astronomy. He wrote from a young age, churning out short stories and poems, and even compiling his own scientific journals, *The Rhode Island Journal of Astronomy* and *The Scientific Gazette*, which he shared with his friends. Although he was born into a relatively wealthy family, the deaths of his father and grandfather during his childhood and adolescence meant Lovecraft and his mother, Sarah Susan Phillips Lovecraft, struggled financially. The young Howard also suffered with periods of ill health, including a nervous breakdown in his teens that caused him to pull out of high school and become somewhat reclusive for several years. After his mother's death in 1921, Howard's two beloved aunts, Lillian and Annie, became the key maternal figures in his life—although in his many letters to them, he often called them his "daughters," and also tended to refer to himself as "Grandpa."

In 1924, Howard married the writer and milliner Sonia Haft Greene, and moved with her to New York, leaving behind his aunts and his beloved hometown. Although he had a lively circle of friends in New York, including a group of fellow writers who became known as the "Kalem Club" (see page 119), Lovecraft detested the city and desperately missed Providence, finally returning there after two years—without his wife, from whom he eventually separated. He lived in Providence for the rest of his short life, writing stories and thousands of letters, and taking frequent trips to explore his beloved New England, until his death at the age of forty-six. Although a number of his stories had been published while he was alive, most notably in the iconic pulp magazine *Weird Tales*, it wasn't until after his death that Lovecraft's work really began to gain attention. Now, he's one of the best-known writers of weird fiction in history.

Interestingly enough, food doesn't tend to feature all that often in Lovecraft's work—generally, his protagonists are too busy frantically trying to evade capture by alarming intergalactic beings—and when it does pop up, the focus is often on sustenance over enjoyment, like the bowl of canned vegetable soup with crackers that the narrator eats in a dingy and unappealing restaurant in "The Shadow over Innsmouth" (see page 20).

While food may not be at the center of Lovecraft's tales, it's interesting to note that in one of his earliest stories, "The Beast in the Cave," which he is thought to have written at the age of just fifteen, he talks about the idea of starving to death as a horrific fate; when trapped in a cave and fearing the approach of a wild beast he believes to be a mountain lion, the narrator says: "Perhaps . . . the Almighty had chosen for me a swifter and more merciful death than that of hunger."

Due in part to his lack of success within his own lifetime, Lovecraft lived very frugally and often expressed a reluctance to spend money on food, preferring to eat as little as possible (see page 57). In general, he tended to stick to bread, cheese, canned foods, coffee, donuts, and ice cream, although he was also very fond of spaghetti (see page 32). Although he occasionally enjoyed fruit, he wasn't a huge vegetable fan. In a 1931 letter, he told his correspondent Vernon Shea: "I like peas & onions, can tolerate cabbage & turnips, am neutral toward cauliflower, have no deep enmity toward carrots, prefer to dodge parsnips & asparagus, shun string beans & brussel sprouts & abominate spinach. I like rhubarb—& am also really fond of baked beans prepared in the ancient New England way."

In this collection, however, we have indulged our inner epicures and explored some more extravagant flavors to truly do justice to the breadth of Lovecraft's boundless imagination. As well as some of the dishes he mentions in his letters, then, this tome contains a wealth of recipes that celebrate his most famous—and terrifying—creations, from creatures found far beneath the waves to visitors from across time and space.

THE DREAM-FEAST OF UNKNOWN KADATH

If you want to prepare a sumptuous repast worthy of a dream-wandering hero like Randolph Carter, try putting together this menu based on all our favorite Dream-Quest themed dishes.

Starter: Spicy Night Gaunt Wings (page 80)

Main dish: Zoog Stroganoff (page 88) paired with Moon-tree Wine (page 142)

Dessert: King Kuranes's Cornish Cream Tea (page 110)

To finish: The Juice of Deeper Slumber (page 154)

THE BANQUET OF CTHULHU

Hold a fishy feast in honor of Cthulhu; just try not to awaken him from his slumbers . . .

Cocktails and nibbles: Cthulhu Tentacles (page 83) paired with Necronomicon Negronis (page 144)

Starter: R'lyeh Pie (page 89)

Main dish: Cthulhu's Squid Spaghetti (page 70)

Dessert: Eldritch Puddings (page 122)

A DAY OF H.P.'S HUMBLE HOME COOKING

If you fancy something a little more reminiscent of Lovecraft's own diet, this menu will see you through a day of eating like our favorite eldritch writer.

Breakfast: Donuts for Breakfast (page 14), served with coffee

Morning snack: Coffee, cheese and crackers

Lunch: Milan's Minestrone (page 32), followed by coffee and ice cream

Dinner: Sonia's Magical Spaghetti (page 75)—or, if you don't have a Sonia, try Lovecraft's tips for a quick beans-on-toast dish on page 60

Kalem Club: Kleiner's Crumb Cake (page 114) and coffee

Breaking Fast

"I am not wedded to certain foods at certain hours," Lovecraft wrote in a 1925 letter to his Aunt Lillian—and it's true that he didn't keep to a typical schedule, often staying up all night drinking coffee and talking with friends, then sleeping in, before writing well into the evening. But whatever time of day you choose to partake of these delicious breakfast treats, there's plenty to enjoy. Celebrate Lovecraft's much-loved hometown with our delicious Providence Pancakes (page 12), or try out the writer's own favorite breakfast, donuts with cheese (page 13). If you choose to sample Zadok's Bootleg Marmalade (pages 20–21), be sure to go for a generous helping: when it came to preserves, Lovecraft once wrote to his friend Vernon Shea: "I like [them] so much that I pile on amounts thicker than the bread that sustains them!" Whatever you choose, be sure to wash it down with plenty of coffee: just the thing to revive you after a sleepless night, whether you stayed up philosophizing with friends, or just couldn't bring yourself to turn off the light after one too many scary stories.

Providence Oatmeal

Before he devoted himself to the weird and wonderful world of his fiction, Lovecraft's first love was undoubtedly his hometown of Providence, Rhode Island. When he moved to New York in 1924, he wrote numerous letters about how much he missed his home, and was over the moon to move back in 1926, after which he remained in Providence for the rest of his life. He dedicated a poem to the town, "Providence," in which he waxes lyrical about the "narrow winding ways" and "leafy hillside." The town often features in his writing, perhaps most notably in *The Case of Charles Dexter Ward*, where "the venerable town" with its "clustered spires, domes, roofs" and "purple hills" provides the backdrop to an unsettling tale of resurrection and necromancy. So enjoy this delicious oatmeal—featuring bananas, which Lovecraft described in a letter to his Aunt Lillian as "an excellent staple"—in honor of this quintessential New England town.

Incredibly fast, easy and healthy. This rich and creamy oatmeal recipe, with bananas and cinnamon sugar, is comfort in a bowl. Oatmeal really is a fantastic canvas for seasonal toppings, so mix it up and get creative with endless sweet and savory flavor options.

SERVES 4–8

Prep + cooking time 25 minutes

4 cups skim or
   low-fat milk
2 cups water
1 teaspoon vanilla extract
pinch of ground cinnamon
pinch of salt
1 cup oats

For the toppings
2 bananas
¼ cup light or dark brown sugar
¼ teaspoon ground cinnamon

1. Put the milk, water, vanilla extract, cinnamon, and salt in a large saucepan over a medium heat, and bring slowly to boil.

2. Stir in the oats, then reduce the heat and simmer gently, stirring occasionally, for 8–10 minutes until creamy and tender.

3. Slice the bananas, then mix together the sugar and cinnamon.

4. Once the oatmeal is cooked, spoon into the bowls, divide the sliced banana among the bowls on top of the oats, and sprinkle with the cinnamon sugar.

Donuts for Breakfast

Lovecraft declared, rather grandly, in a 1929 letter to his Aunt Lillian: "Breakfast, of course, I never eat." This wasn't entirely true; he did occasionally indulge in a morning repast, and one of his favorite breakfast treats is a bit of an odd one: donuts and cheese. In a letter to his other aunt, Annie, he tells her: "For breakfast . . . I uniformly have my favorite Downyflake doughnuts & cheese," referring to a local donut shop. So it you fancy a truly Lovecraftian start to your day, try pairing these tasty donuts with a slice or two of your favorite cheese . . .

Who doesn't love a donut? And, although they take a bit of time, homemade ones are far and away the best. Enjoy the donuts right away while still warm.

MAKES 10
Prep + cooking time 30 minutes, plus proofing

For the dough
2¾ cups white bread flour, plus extra for dusting
½ teaspoon salt
¼ cup superfine sugar
1¼ teaspoons instant yeast
2 tablespoons unsalted butter, melted
1 cup milk, gently warmed
2 teaspoons vanilla extract
1 large egg, beaten

To finish
½ cup superfine sugar
1 teaspoon ground cinnamon
vegetable oil, for deep-frying

1. Sift the flour into a large bowl. Add the remaining dry ingredients, gently mix, and then gradually add the wet ingredients. Mix to form a rough dough.

2. Tip out onto a floured surface and knead for 10 minutes, or until the dough is not sticky and slightly springy to the touch. Add more flour as necessary.

3. Place the dough in a clean, lightly oiled bowl, cover with oiled plastic wrap, and let rise in a warm place for 1½ hours or until doubled in volume.

4. Turn out onto a floured surface and shape into 10 equal balls on a large, greased baking sheet. Cover loosely with oiled plastic wrap and let rise in a warm place for 30–40 minutes or until almost doubled in size.

5. Sprinkle the sugar and cinnamon on a plate. Put 3 inches of oil in a large saucepan and heat until a small piece of bread sizzles on the surface and turns pale golden in about 30 seconds.

6. Fry the donuts, three or four at a time, for about 3-4 minutes, turning them once until golden on both sides. Drain with a slotted spoon onto several sheets of paper towels. Roll the donuts in the cinnamon sugar while still warm.

Sonia's "Edible" Bran Muffins

In 1924, Lovecraft got married to Sonia Greene, a milliner and writer with whom he moved to New York City. His beloved aunts didn't approve of the relationship, which may be why he and Sonia married in secret. Howard broke the news to his aunts in a letter a few days later, in which he enthused about his new wife's cooking, saying it was "the last word in perfection," and adding proudly that his bride "even makes edible bran muffins!" High praise indeed!

If Lovecraft's description of Sonia's muffins sounds a little lacking in romance, it's nothing compared to how they spent their wedding night. He had a deadline to meet, and the pair of them spent their first night as husband and wife frantically typing to get it all done. It was, he noted with satisfaction, "truly, a most practical and industrious honeymoon."

The secret to baking the best muffins is simple—don't overmix the batter, as this will make them tough. Fold the wet ingredients into the dry, and mix gently and briefly. Try these sweet treats with raspberries in place of the blueberries.

MAKES 12

Prep + cooking time 30 minutes

2 cups all-purpose flour
1 cup bran
1 teaspoon baking powder
1 teaspoon baking soda
3 eggs
1 teaspoon vanilla extract
1 cup buttermilk
¼ cup peanut oil
1 cup blueberries

1. Lightly grease a 12-cup nonstick muffin pan or line the muffin pan with baking cups.

2. In a large bowl, mix together the dry ingredients until well combined. Break the eggs into a bowl and beat lightly, then add the vanilla extract, buttermilk, and oil.

3. Pour the egg mixture into the dry ingredients, add the blueberries, and fold gently using a large metal spoon just until barely combined.

4. Spoon the batter evenly among the muffin cups.

5. Bake at 350°F for 18–20 minutes, until risen, golden, and firm. Remove from the oven and transfer to a cooling rack to cool slightly before serving warm.

Shantak Eggs with Spinach

The Dream-Quest of Unknown Kadath is one of Lovecraft's longest works, and sees Randolph Carter on a determined mission to find a "marvellous city" he has repeatedly dreamed about. Carter is a recurring protagonist of Lovecraft's, appearing in seven of his works, with his first appearance coming in "The Statement of Randolph Carter," a retelling of a nightmare Lovecraft had in which Carter takes on the role of Lovecraft himself. In another story, "The Unnameable," Carter is briefly revealed to be a writer, and it's easy to see a link between Carter and his creator—both are creative, self-contained men given to dreaming—but Lovecraft expert and biographer S. T. Joshi has said that Carter is "not so much a character as a fictional exponent of [Lovecraft's] philosophical outlook." In *The Dream-Quest*, Carter descends deep into the land of dream, where he encounters various weird and wonderful creatures, including "the rumoured shantak-bird" known for its "colossal and rich-flavoured eggs." Though the birds are alarming, it's clear their eggs are highly sought after and would make a delicious and dreamy breakfast.

A perfect Sunday brunch for two that combines soft-set eggs with sweet leeks and wilted spinach, this health-packed dish works well for a quick midweek dinner too.

SERVES 2

Prep + cooking time 15 minutes

2 tablespoons butter

1 leek, trimmed, cleaned, and thinly sliced

¼ teaspoon dried red pepper flakes

10 cups baby spinach leaves

2 eggs

3 tablespoons plain yogurt

pinch of ground paprika

salt and black pepper

1. Heat the butter in a skillet, add the leek and red pepper flakes, and cook over medium–high heat for 4–5 minutes, until softened. Add the spinach and season well, then toss and cook for 2 minutes, until wilted.

2. Make two wells in the center of the vegetables and break the eggs into the well. Cook over low heat for 2–3 minutes, until the eggs are set. Spoon the yogurt on top and sprinkle with the paprika.

Not-quite-20-minute Eggs

When he wasn't indulging in a morning donut or denying the existence of breakfast altogether, Lovecraft might have a more traditional start to his day by eating eggs. However, true to his quirky nature, he seems to have had a very particular way of preparing them. In a letter to his Aunt Lillian, he boasts of having made his own breakfast: "a 20-minute egg which I cookt with vast finesse." Given that in other letters he expresses a fondness for hard-boiled eggs, we can only assume that his 20-minute version was very hard-boiled. Try these for a slightly less rock-solid option.

Ah, the comfort of dipping a crisp finger of toast into a perfectly cooked egg yolk. Here, this favorite is given a hint of grown-up heat by adding mustard. For a luxury variation, you could replace the toast with freshly cooked asparagus spears—just boil or steam for 2 minutes so they keep their crunch.

SERVES 4

Prep + cooking time 10 minutes

2 teaspoons whole-grain mustard, or to taste

¼ cup unsalted butter, softened

4 large eggs

4 thick slices of white bread

black pepper

microgreens or baby herb leaves, to garnish (optional)

1. Beat the mustard, butter, and pepper together in a small bowl.

2. Cook the eggs in a saucepan of boiling water for 4–5 minutes. Meanwhile, toast the bread, then butter one side with the mustard butter, and cut into fingers.

3. Serve the eggs with the mustard fingers and garnished with microgreens or baby herb leaves, if desired.

Zadok's Bootleg Marmalade

Lovecraft was, according to philosopher Jan B. W. Pedersen, a "dramatic teetotaller," and the dangers of alcohol are explored in several of his tales, including "Old Bugs" and "The Quest of Iranon." In one such occurence, in *The Shadow Over Innsmouth*, the narrator, who is on a sightseeing tour of New England, makes an ill-advised stop in the strange town of Innsmouth, a place known for its unusual-looking inhabitants and abundance of fish. He meets the local drunkard, the ninety-six-year-old Zadok Allen, who he learns is "unable to resist any offer of his favourite poison." Eager to discover more about the strange town, the narrator duly plies Zadok with bootleg whiskey, and in return learns a terrifying tale. A warning, perhaps, from Lovecraft. Here, at least, the whiskey is used to flavor a tasty marmalade, which perhaps he would have found more appealing.

It's important that the jars are sterilized—they should be still hot and completely dry before adding the marmalade. You can sterilize by putting the jars and lids through the hottest cycle of the dishwasher without detergent, or by placing them in a large pan, covering with cold water, and bringing to a boil over high heat for 20 minutes.

An easy way to tell if the marmalade has reached setting point (see below) is to drop a teaspoon of it onto a saucer that's been chilled in the freezer. The marmalade will quickly cool to room temperature. Push it gently with your finger—the skin will wrinkle if it's ready. If it's not, return the marmalade to the heat, boil it again, and retest in a few minutes.

MAKES 4 JARS

Prep + cooking time 2 hours

6 Seville or bitter oranges
   (about 2 pounds)

juice of 1 lemon

5 cups granulated sugar, warmed

¼ cup whiskey

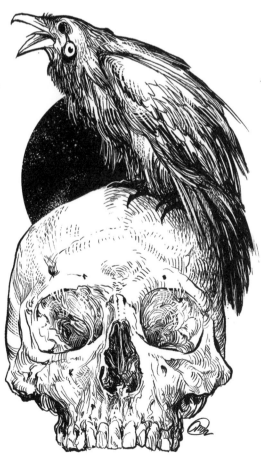

1. Add the whole oranges to a large saucepan in a single layer. Just cover with cold water, bring to a boil, cover with a lid, and cook gently for 1 hour, or until the oranges can be pierced easily with a sharp knife. Let cool.

2. While the oranges are cooling, warm the sugar. Pour the sugar into a heatproof bowl, and into an oven preheated to 275°F, stirring the sugar once or twice while it warms. The sugar should take about 30 minutes to warm up.

3. Remove the oranges from the pan with a slotted spoon, draining well. Reserve 3¾ cups of the cooking liquid. Halve the oranges, scoop out the seeds, and reserve. Cut the oranges into thin slices. Add the slices to the pan with the seeds tied in a square of cheesecloth, the measured cooking liquid, and the lemon juice. Simmer over medium heat for 10 minutes, until the orange slices are tender.

4. Add the sugar and heat gently, stirring occasionally, until the sugar has dissolved. Bring to a boil, then boil rapidly until setting point is reached (20–25 minutes, see opposite). Lift out the cheesecloth bag, squeezing well. Stir in the whiskey and let cool for 10 minutes. Ladle into sterilized jars, working with one at a time. Fill each jar to ¼ inch from the top. Using a plastic spatula, disperse any air bubbles. Repeat with the remaining jars and seal immediately.

Yog-Sothoth Pots

Yog-Sothoth is a terrifying and all-knowing Outer God who appears in *The Case of Charles Dexter Ward* and "The Dunwich Horror." In a 1926 letter to his friend James F. Morton, Lovecraft drew a detailed "family tree" for many of the entities he'd created: on this, Yog-Sothoth is listed as the spawn of "The Nameless Mist." Lovecraft is notorious for not quite describing some of his monstrous creations; his narrators are often struck dumb or driven mad by what they see, and left unable to put into words the horrors they have witnessed. Yog-Sothoth seems to invoke this kind of reaction, and is described in only the vaguest of terms as being formed of "malignant globes." Being a timeless being made of evil spheres doesn't stop Yog-Sothoth from breeding with a human woman, however, and the resulting offspring are the key figures in "The Dunwich Horror."

Super-easy and super-fast, these pretty breakfast treats use frozen fruit for extra convenience, though you could use fresh if you have it. You could also add a little finely chopped mint for a refreshing burst of flavor and swap out the granola for mixed pumpkin and sunflower seeds.

SERVES 4

Prep time 10 minutes

3½ cups frozen mixed berries, thawed
juice of 1 orange
⅓ cup honey
2 cups vanilla yogurt
½ cup granola

1. Process half the berries with the orange juice and honey in a blender or food processor until smooth. Transfer to a bowl and stir in the remaining berries.

2. Divide one-third of the berry mixture among four individual dessert glasses or small bowls. Top with half the yogurt. Layer with half the remaining berry mixture and top with the remaining yogurt.

3. Top with the remaining berry mixture and sprinkle the granola on top just before serving.

H. Peach Pancakes & Ice Cream

Lovecraft's fondness for ice cream is no secret, and he even made a habit of indulging in it at breakfast time, telling his aunt, "My breakfast is a large cheese sandwich, coffee & ice-cream at a United Cigar Store lunch counter." In slightly healthier moments, he enjoyed fresh fruit, telling Lillian in one of his letters, "I like peaches best." In fact, in another letter, he mentions "growing addicted" to peach pie. It seems appropriate to combine two of his great loves, ice cream and peaches, for a truly decadent morning feast.

These crêpes make a wonderful brunch for a special occasion, and kids will be excited that they get to eat them topped with ice cream! For a healthier spin, you could opt for thick plain yogurt instead. Use whatever fruit you have in the bowl: sliced bananas and fresh berries work really well.

SERVES 4

Prep + cooking time 20 minutes

1 cup whole-wheat flour (or half whole-wheat and half all-purpose white flour)

pinch of salt

1 egg

1 tablespoon butter, melted

⅔ cup milk

sunflower oil, for frying

3 ripe peaches, pitted and sliced, or sliced canned peaches

4 scoops of vanilla ice cream (optional)

¼ cup maple syrup

1. Place the flour and salt in a mixing bowl. Make a well in the center and break the egg into it. Add the melted butter and one-quarter of the milk. Mix with a wooden spoon or handheld mixer, adding more milk as the batter thickens, until all the milk is used. Beat well to make a smooth batter.

2. Heat a small, nonstick skillet until hot and lightly grease with a little sunflower oil. Pour in about two tablespoons of batter, swirling the skillet so the batter evenly coats the bottom of the skillet. Cook for 1 minute, until golden underneath, then turn over and cook the other side until golden. Slide out onto a plate and keep warm. Repeat with the remaining batter to make eight thin pancakes.

3. Fold the pancakes into quarters and serve with the peach slices, a scoop of ice cream (if desired), and a drizzle of maple syrup.

Fueling the Imagination: Coffee

"We live on a placid island of ignorance in the midst of black seas of infinity, and it was not meant that we should voyage far."

—*"The Call of Cthulhu"*

As a teetotaller, Lovecraft's favorite drink seems to have been coffee, and in his letters he talks about "tak[ing] coffee during the small hours" during all-night sessions with his friends, especially those in the Kalem Club. It is easy to imagine this group of like-minded intellectuals, gathering in each other's studies or in brightly lit New York diners, and comparing notes and swapping ideas over cups of steaming coffee. As we learned on page 119, Lovecraft wasn't confident in his ability to make his own, so he bought a pail to collect it from a café and bring it home to serve to guests. Perhaps this was just in an effort to provide his friends with the very best, however, as in other letters to his Aunt Lillian he seems to be making an effort to learn how to make it himself: "Sunday & Monday I [spent] perfecting my household technique and coffee-making art."

And how did Lovecraft take his coffee? Given his undeniable sweet tooth, it's no surprise to learn that he enjoyed it with sugar. In a 1936 letter to Mrs. Fritz Leiber, he told her: "I never employ less than four teaspoons in an average cup of coffee," although this may have been down to the probable bitterness of the cheap coffee available to him at the time.

He was also partial to Postum, a caffeine-free coffee substitute made from powdered roasted wheat bran and molasses, which he drank with condensed milk, telling his Aunt Annie he felt that this would make for "an intensive health-food diet! I ought to feel new waves of health coming over me!"

As well as fueling late-night writing sessions (and perhaps causing a few unsettling dreams that may have led to ghoulish inspiration), coffee also makes an appearance in Lovecraft's fiction. In "The Whisperer in the Darkness," Wilmarth arrives at Akeley's home and is served sandwiches, cake, cheese, and coffee while his whispering host sits in shadow in the next room. Lovecraft writes: "I poured myself a liberal cup of coffee, but found that the culinary standard had suffered a lapse in this one detail. My first spoonful revealed a faintly unpleasant, acrid taste, so that I did not take more." Wilmarth pours it away; later, he realizes the drink had been drugged by alien creatures who seem hell-bent on cutting out the brains of Earth's intellectuals. Perhaps he should have asked for Postum instead.

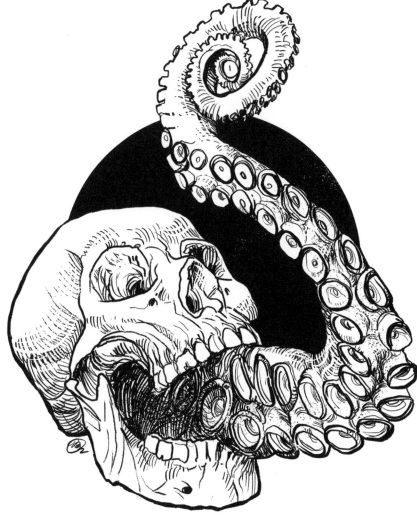

Lighter Bites

The lighter meals in this chapter would no doubt have appealed to the frugal and reserved Lovecraft. We've included no fewer than five soups in honor of his fondness for that humble dish, although we've suggested making your own rather than going for canned, as Howard usually did. He wasn't a particularly keen cook, once writing to his Aunt Lillian that "I eat so simply that I seldom have to do any dishwashing beyond a single plate, or cup & saucer, plus one or two metallic utensils." However, when he liked a dish, he really liked it—as you'll see when you try Milan's Minestrone on page 32. The offerings in this chapter celebrate some of his most sinister stories, including "Cool Air" (Dr. Muñoz's Oysters, page 41) and "The Vault" (Coffin Loaf, page 54). Fans of Lovecraft's most famous monsters will be thrilled by the Mi-Go Soup on pages 39–40 and the Sushi of the Old Ones on pages 45–47, while the Shunned Fungus and Garlic Crostini on page 48 is sure to give you nightmares.

Kalos's Olives

"On the verdant slope of Mount Maenalus, in Arcadia, there stands an olive grove about the ruins of a villa. Close by is a tomb . . . at one end of that tomb, its curious roots displacing the time-stained blocks of Pentelic marble, grows an unnaturally large olive tree of oddly repellent shape; so like to some grotesque man, or death-distorted body of a man, that the country folk fear to pass it at night when the moon shines faintly through the crooked boughs."

So opens Lovecraft's short story "The Tree," which tells the tale of two sculptors, Kalos and Musides, who are invited to compete in a sculpture competition by the Tyrant of Syracuse. As the pair work on their respective designs, Kalos grows sickly and weak, and Musides cares for him. On his deathbed, Kalos asks his friends to bury twigs from his beloved olive trees by his grave, and soon after his death, a new tree takes root there, growing rapidly. Musides finishes his statue, but when the Tyrant's men come to collect it, they find the sculpture shattered beneath a huge branch of the olive tree—and Musides nowhere to be seen.

Zesty citrus and the slightly sweet licorice flavor of fennel seeds take everyday olives to a new level. They taste even better if allowed to steep overnight to absorb the flavors. Serve with pre-dinner drinks or as part of a mezze platter.

SERVES 6

Prep + cooking time 5 minutes, plus marinating overnight (optional)

2 teaspoons fennel seeds
finely grated zest and juice of ½ lemon
finely grated zest and juice of ¼ orange
⅓ cup olive oil
4 cups mixed olives

1. Put the fennel seeds into a small, dry skillet and toast for 30 seconds, until they start to pop and emit an aroma. Remove from the pan and roughly crush.

2. Mix together the fennel seeds, lemon and orange zests and juices, and oil in a nonmetallic bowl, then stir in the olives. Serve immediately, or cover and let marinate overnight in a cool place before serving.

Cypress Swamp Soup

"The Statement of Randolph Carter" is one of Lovecraft's shorter offerings, but it still packs a weird and haunting punch. In it, Carter relates how he and his friend Harley Warren made their way toward Big Cypress Swamp late one night, armed with "electric lanterns, spades, and a curious coil of wire with attached instruments." Carter is found "alone and dazed" beside the swamp in the morning, and reveals that Warren, a mystic and collector of rare books, had descended into a tomb in a nearby cemetery while Carter waited above. Instead of returning, though, Warren cries out to him, "Carter! for the love of God, put the slab back on and get out of this if you can! Quick!" as he meets some awful fate below the surface. This soup, inspired by the greenish swamp that frames the story, features one of the only green vegetables Lovecraft seemed able to stomach—"I've slowly come to like peas if they are small & young," he wrote to his aunt, "but cannot bear string beans or asparagus."

This vibrant and versatile soup is equally delicious warm or chilled. You can change it up by adding 2 tablespoons of chopped mint before you puree it, and serving each bowl garnished with a mint sprig.

SERVES 4

Prep + cooking time 25 minutes

1 tablespoon butter

bunch of scallions, chopped

2½ pounds fresh peas, shelled, or 3 cups frozen peas

3 cups vegetable stock

2 tablespoons thick plain yogurt or light cream

nutmeg

1 tablespoon chopped chives, to garnish

1. Melt the butter in a large pan and soften the scallions, but do not allow them to brown. Add the peas to the pan with the stock. Bring to a boil and simmer for about 5 minutes for frozen peas, but for up to 15 minutes for fresh peas, until they are cooked. Be careful not to overcook fresh peas or they will lose their flavor.

2. Remove from the heat and puree in a blender or food processor. Add the yogurt or cream and grate in a little nutmeg. Reheat gently if necessary, and serve sprinkled with chives.

Milan's Minestrone

One of Lovecraft's favorite eateries in New York was Milan, an Italian restaurant where he frequently dined on his "favorite comestibles," spaghetti and minestrone soup. Minestrone occupied a special place in his heart. In one 1925 letter to his aunts, he rhapsodizes: "This thick & nutritious soup is part of every full Italian dinner . . . & I gorged myself unstintedly on a full tureen; thus obtaining a complete & incomparably fine meal for 15c." He insists that no other restaurant can make minestrone quite like that he enjoys at Milan, but short of a time machine to take you to 1920s New York, this recipe is your next best option.

*This hearty winter warmer is great for using up whatever is lurking in the fridge.
You can replace the cabbage with collard greens or kale and it's great with zucchini
added too. It tastes even better the next day and freezes well, so you could double the
quantities and make a big batch.*

SERVES 4
Prep + cooking time 30 minutes

2 tablespoons olive oil

1 onion, chopped

1 carrot, peeled and chopped

1 celery stalk, chopped

1 teaspoon tomato paste

2 garlic cloves, finely chopped

13-ounce can diced tomatoes

3 cups hot chicken or vegetable stock

2 thyme sprigs, leaves stripped

4 ounces ditalini pasta

13-ounce can cannellini beans, rinsed
   and drained

½ head of Savoy cabbage, shredded

salt and pepper

grated Parmesan cheese, to serve

1. Heat the oil in a large saucepan, add the onion, carrot, and celery, and cook over low heat for 10 minutes until really soft.

2. Stir in the tomato paste and garlic, then add the tomatoes, stock, and thyme and simmer for 10 minutes.

3. Add the pasta and beans to the soup and cook for an additional 10 minutes or until the pasta is cooked through. Add the cabbage 5 minutes before the end of the cooking time and cook until tender. Season well with salt and pepper.

4. Ladle into serving bowls and serve sprinkled with the Parmesan.

Enchanted Turkey & Chestnut Soup

Although he often dined quite simply, Lovecraft occasionally indulged in a feast, and in one 1924 letter to his aunts, he describes a hearty meal enjoyed for Thanksgiving with his friends Samuel Loveman, a poet and playwright, and George Kirk, a bookseller and publisher. The meal consisted of: "Enchanted soup—apotheosized roast turkey with dressing of chestnuts & . . . rare spices and savory herbs," along with "cauliflower with cryptical creaming" and "gravy for which Apicius strove & Lucullus sigh'd in vain"— and much more besides. It was, Lovecraft enthuses: "All the glory of earth sublimated in one transcendent repast—one divides one's life into periods of before & after having consumed—or even smelled or dream'd of—such a meal!"

High praise indeed, even if our favorite writer of the weird and wonderful was sometimes prone to a touch of hyperbole. It certainly makes a change from some of the more frugal meals that Howard tended to consume at home (in fact, in the same letter, he refers to the fact that his aunts have promised to send him "a box of turkey" in the mail, so perhaps they too felt he needed a few more treats in his life). It's easy to imagine the table groaning with the weight of all this delicious food as the friends enjoyed their meal. After they'd eaten, "in the torpor which follows such orgies of nourishment," Lovecraft read aloud some of his latest stories to round out the evening.

If a multiple-course turkey feast isn't an option, this delectable soup combines some of the key elements of that celebrated meal. It is best enjoyed by candlelight, with your favorite Lovecraftian tales on hand so you can take it in turns to give a post-meal literary reading.

A great way to make sure that not a scrap of the Thanksgiving or Christmas turkey is wasted. For a corn take on this, omit the chestnuts and instead add a drained 11-ounce can of corn kernels at the end of the cooking time. Don't worry too much about the quantity of turkey meat in the recipe—just use whatever you have.

SERVES 6

Prep + cooking time 4 hours

1 turkey carcass

2 onions, finely chopped

2 carrots, peeled and finely chopped

2 celery stalks, finely chopped

7½ cups water

2 cups cooked turkey meat, cut into bite-size pieces

2 tablespoons oil

2 large potatoes, diced

15-ounce can whole chestnuts in brine, drained

3 tablespoons sherry or port

salt and black pepper

1. Break the turkey carcass into pieces and place in a large saucepan with half the onions, carrots and celery stalks, and the seasoning. Add the measured water and bring to a boil. Cover and simmer for 3 hours. Add extra water as necessary.

2. Remove the carcass and vegetables, and discard. Strain the stock and add the turkey meat.

3. Heat the oil in the rinsed-out pan, then add the potatoes and the remaining onions, carrots, and celery. Cook gently, stirring, for 5 minutes.

4. Pour in the turkey stock and bring to a boil. Simmer for 20 minutes, then add the chestnuts and sherry or port. Reheat and check the seasoning before serving.

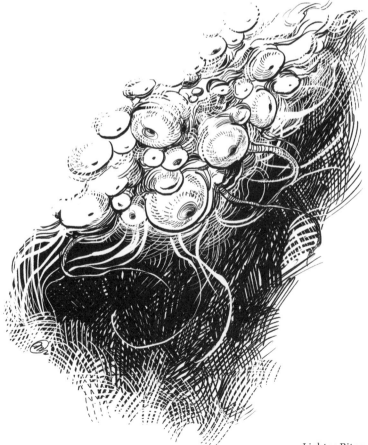

Olmstead's Vegetable Soup

Lovecraft's horror of all things oceanic can be seen in many of his tales, including, of course, "The Call of Cthulhu." The writer once told his friend Donald Wandrei: "I have hated fish and feared the sea and everything connected to it since I was two years old." In *The Shadow Over Innsmouth*, much of the sense of doom in the story comes from the sinister town's closeness to the sea—and what lives there. We're told the whole place is pervaded by "the most nauseous fishy odour imaginable," and there's a distinctly marine look to some of the locals. Having interrogated the town drunkard, Zadok (see page 20), the hapless narrator Robert Olmstead (whose name is never actually given in the story, but has been found among Lovecraft's notes) finds himself stranded in Innsmouth for the night and is forced to seek sustenance at its single "dismal restaurant." There, he is served by "a stooped, narrow-headed man with staring, unwinking eyes." Unsurprisingly, Olmstead decides not to sample any of the local fishy delicacies, and opts instead for a veggie soup: "It relieved me to find that much was evidently served from cans and packages. A bowl of vegetable soup with crackers was enough for me."

This choice perhaps was inspired by what we know, from Lovecraft's letters, of his own fondness of the convenience and frugality of canned foods, but this tasty spinach and red lentil soup is much more appealing. To enjoy in true Innsmouth style, serve with crackers and a side of mounting dread.

Comforting on a cold, gray day, this spicy vegetarian soup is packed with good-for-you ingredients including antioxidant ginger, fiber-filled lentils, and iron-rich spinach. For a vegan-friendly soup, opt for nondairy versions of the half-and-half and yogurt.

Continued overleaf →

SERVES 4

Prep + cooking time 30 minutes

1⅓ cups dried red lentils

3 tablespoons sunflower oil

1 large onion, finely chopped

2 garlic cloves, crushed

1-inch piece fresh ginger root, grated

1 red chili, seeded and chopped, plus
  extra to garnish (optional)

1 tablespoon medium curry powder

1¼ cups hot vegetable stock

¾ cup canned tomatoes

3½ cups baby leaf spinach

½ cup chopped cilantro, plus extra
  to garnish

½ cup half-and-half mixed with
  ¼ teaspoon vanilla extract

salt and black pepper

¼ cup plain yogurt, to serve

1. Put the lentils into a medium saucepan and cover with 4 cups of cold water. Bring to a boil, skim off the scum as it rises to the surface, and let simmer for 10 minutes, until the lentils are tender and just falling apart. Remove from the heat, cover, and set aside.

2. Meanwhile, heat the oil in a large saucepan, add the onion, and cook gently for 5 minutes. Add the garlic, ginger, and chili and cook for 2 minutes. Stir in the curry powder and ½ teaspoon black pepper and cook for an additional 2 minutes.

3. Add the stock, the lentils and their cooking liquid, the tomatoes, spinach, and cilantro and season with salt. Cover and simmer for 5 minutes, then add the vanilla-flavored half-and-half.

4. Process the mixture with an immersion blender until the soup is almost smooth.

5. Ladle the soup into four bowls and garnish each with a spoonful of yogurt, the remaining cilantro, freshly ground black pepper, and finely chopped red chili, if desired.

Mi-Go Soup

The Mi-Go, also called "the Outer Ones," first appear in "The Whisperer in Darkness." They are strange, fungus-like extraterrestrial creatures from Yuggoth, a recently discovered new planet in the solar system. Interestingly, the discovery of Pluto was officially announced in March 1930; Lovecraft began writing "The Whisperer in Darkness" in February of that year, and finished it in September. So while Lovecraft had already formed his idea before the announcement was made, writer Fred S. Lubnow says it "obviously had a huge impact on the development of the story." The Mi-Go, we learn, can remove the brains of humans in order to take them on voyages through space. This tasty mushroom and miso soup should be a little more appealing than these strange alien creatures—and the miso adds a touch of umami, that elusive fifth flavor that's as hard to capture as the Mi-Go themselves, who don't even show up on film when photographed.

A staple of Japanese cuisine, ultra-savory miso paste is made with fermented soybeans. It forms the basis of this quick and easy vegan soup which, here, is served with delicious sticky rice for a more substantial meal.

Continued overleaf →

SERVES 4

Prep + cooking time 25 minutes, plus soaking time

For the rice
1½ cups glutinous rice

For the soup
7½ cups vegetable stock
2 tablespoons miso paste
2 cups sliced shiitake mushrooms
7 ounces firm tofu, cubed

1. Wash the rice in several changes of water and drain. Put it in a large mixing bowl, cover with cold water, and allow to soak for about 1 hour. Drain the rice and wash it again. Put in a saucepan with 1¼ cups water and bring to a simmer. Cover and cook very gently for 20 minutes or until the water is absorbed and the rice is tender. Add a little more water if the pan dries out before the rice is cooked.

2. Meanwhile, to make the soup, put the stock in a saucepan and heat until simmering.

3. Add the miso paste, shiitake mushrooms, and tofu to the stock and simmer gently for 5 minutes. Serve immediately with the rice.

Dr. Muñoz's Oysters

Lovecraft's short story "Cool Air" is one of his simpler offerings—no otherworldly creatures or complex hierarchies of Outer Gods—but it's no less unsettling. Lovecraft scholar Robert H. Waugh describes the tale as "one of Lovecraft's first experiments in moving the weird tale into the broad genre of science fiction." The story is somewhat unusual for Lovecraft in that it is set very firmly in the real world, in New York—in fact, Waugh explains that the apartment building was inspired by the brownstone on West 14th Street where Lovecraft's friend George Kirk resided. In the story, the narrator lives in a rented room below the retired Dr. Muñoz, who spends his time engaged in a series of unusual experiments involving ammonia and other substances. At one point, ammonia even drips through the ceiling into the narrator's room, a moment that Waugh notes echoes the scene in Lovecraft's "The Picture in the House" where blood seeps through the ceiling from the floor above. The doctor's apartment is kept at an unusually cold temperature—a treatment, he says, for an illness he has had for many years. When the doctor's air-conditioning system fails during a spell of warm weather, the narrator embarks on a frantic mission to seek out enough ice to fill a bath for Dr. Muñoz, and a repairman for the air conditioning. With the temperature in the apartment growing steadily higher, the narrator returns to discover "a dark, slimy trail"—and the horrible truth about just what that strange illness of the doctor's was.

These delicious oysters served on ice make the perfect pairing for this chilling tale.

A simple shallot vinaigrette is the preferred French accompaniment for fresh oysters. It's so easy to make and a perfect foil for the oysters. Spoon a little over each oyster and serve on a bed of ice as a luxurious appetizer or light meal.

SERVES 4

Prep time 10 minutes

2 shallots, finely diced
¼ cup sherry vinegar
¼ cup olive oil
juice of 1 lemon
2 tablespoons chopped parsley
24 shucked oysters

1. Mix together the shallots, sherry vinegar, olive oil, lemon juice, and parsley in a bowl.

2. Spoon over 24 shucked oysters and serve on a bed of ice.

Whispering Crab Cakes

Fritz Leiber Jr. wrote of Lovecraft: "He shifted the focus of supernatural dread from man and his little world and his gods to the stars and the black and unplumbed gulfs of intergalactic space. To do this effectively, he created a new kind of horror story and new ways to tell it." Perhaps one of the best examples of this is "The Whisperer in Darkness," a chilling tale of an alien species arriving on Earth having traveled across the vastness of space. These creatures, the Mi-Go, are part-fungus (see page 39), but they're also, strangely enough, part-crustacean. We are told they "were a sort of huge, light-red crab with many pairs of legs and two great bat-like wings." If these mushroom-crab mash-up monsters have alarmed you, soothe your nerves with some fragrant cilantro-spiked crab cakes.

Golden and crispy on the outside, soft and sweet on the inside, these crab cakes make a lovely light meal with the spicy dipping sauce and crisp salad leaves alongside for contrast. Serve the crab cakes as soon as they're cooked.

SERVES 4

Prep + cooking time 30 minutes

10 ounces potatoes, peeled and chopped

12 ounces fresh white crabmeat

3 scallions, sliced

handful of cilantro, finely chopped

good squeeze of lime juice

½ chili, seeded and finely chopped

1 egg yolk

3 tablespoons cornmeal

2 tablespoons vegetable oil

salt and black pepper

mixed leaf salad

lime wedge

For the chili dipping sauce

⅓ cup superfine sugar

2 red chilies, seeded and chopped

1 lemongrass stalk, sliced

1 garlic clove, sliced

zest and juice of 1 lime

1 fresh ginger root, finely chopped

1. Cook the potatoes in a saucepan of salted boiling water for 15 minutes or until tender. Drain well, return to the pan, and mash. Leave to cool. Stir in all the remaining ingredients except the cornmeal and oil.

2. Put the cornmeal on a plate, shape the crab mixture into eight cakes, and coat in the cornmeal. Cover and chill for 20 minutes.

3. Meanwhile, make the dipping sauce. Place the sugar and 4 tablespoons of water in a saucepan, heat until the sugar has dissolved, then bubble until it turns a caramel color. Stir in the red chilies, lemongrass, garlic, lime zest and juice, and ginger root. Remove from the heat, pour into a serving dish, and let cool.

4. Heat the oil in a large skillet, add the cakes, and fry for 2–3 minutes on each side until golden. Serve with the chili dipping sauce, lime wedges, and a mixed leaf salad.

The Great Race Crab Cones

*T*he *Shadow Out of Time* is a time-bending, head-spinning tale of mind-swapping, in which the narrator, Nathaniel Peaslee, comes to realize that he has, for five years, had his mind switched with that of a member of an alien species known as the "Great Race," leaving him with strange half-memories of their world. Writer and Lovecraft expert John Salonia says the tale could be seen as an update on the myth of the dybbuk, "a disembodied human spirit that takes possession of a living person's body," or alternatively, as "a science fiction analogue of demonic possession." The theme of body- or mind-swapping is explored in another of Lovecraft's stories, "The Thing on the Doorstep," but *The Shadow Out of Time* is notable for its sheer scope—Peaslee doesn't just find himself occupying the body of a different species, but one in an entirely different time. The bizarre creatures of the Great Race are described as ten-foot-tall and ten-foot-wide "enormous iridescent cones." These delectable crab cones might not be quite as big, but they make a perfect opening to an eldritch feast.

Make dinner a fun build-your-own affair with these delicious cones—children will love assembling theirs! Delicate crab pairs beautifully with creamy, heart-healthy avocado in this recipe, but if seafood isn't your thing, you could replace the crabmeat with 3½ ounces finely shredded smoked chicken breast.

SERVES 4

Prep + cooking time 25 minutes, plus resting

For the rice

1 cup sushi rice

1 cup plus 2 tablespoons water

⅓ cup rice vinegar

2 tablespoons superfine sugar

½ teaspoon salt

For the filling

6 sheets of nori

1 avocado

juice of 1 lemon

Japanese soy sauce

wasabi paste

Japanese pickled ginger

4 ounces crabmeat, cooked and shelled

1. Cook the rice following the instructions on page 47.

2. Cut each sheet of nori into four pieces.

3. Peel the avocado and slice it into strips. Sprinkle with the lemon juice.

4. Place the soy sauce, wasabi paste, and pickled ginger into separate small bowls.

5. Arrange the nori sheets, avocado strips, and crabmeat on a plate.

6. Let everyone make their own cones by spreading rice on the nori sheets and adding a touch of wasabi, and a little garnish, before rolling them into cones and dipping in the soy sauce.

Sushi of the Old Ones

Lovecraft had long been obsessed with the Antarctic, and in *At the Mountains of Madness*, he indulged this fascination in true Lovecraftian style—with a hefty dose of blood-chilling horror. The novella chronicles the experiences of William Dyer, a member of the Miskatonic Antarctic Expedition. The group's biologist, Lake, leads a sub-expedition away from the main group, and radios back to say his team has found mountains taller than any others on Earth, and the frozen remains of some strange creatures with gray, barrel-shaped bodies, serrated wings, and tentacles. Unusually for Lovecraft, who often leaves a sense of the unknown about his monstrous creations, these beings are described in great detail in the form of a lengthy radio report from Lake. As writer Michel Houellebecq notes, "If there is a tone one does not expect to find in the horror story, it's that of a dissection report." Although the lengthy, precise descriptions could be dull to read, the juxtaposition of this scientific, pragmatic tone with the horror of what is being described is chilling. Houellebecq explains: "By forcefully introducing the language and concepts of scientific sectors . . . [Lovecraft] has exploded the casing of the horror story."

When radio contact is lost, Dyer leads a rescue party in search of the sub-expedition, and finds the camp destroyed and their comrades butchered "in the most curious, cold-blooded and inhuman fashion." Dyer and a colleague head into the mountains and find a vast, abandoned stone city full of wall carvings that tell the history of an ancient race: the Old Ones. Among the many strange things they discover, they learn about the Old Ones' diets: "Though able, like vegetables, to derive nourishment from inorganic substances, they vastly preferred organic and especially animal food," Dyer tells us, adding that "they ate uncooked marine life under the sea." These creatures may have been on the odd-looking side, but they were clearly highly intelligent, so why not take their lead and try a little of this tasty sushi?

You'll need a bamboo sushi mat for this one. Rolling sushi neatly takes a bit of practice but there are a few simple tips for success: don't overfill the roll, as it will fall apart; allow an inch of nori without rice so you can close your roll; and make sure the rough side of the nori faces upward.

Continued overleaf →

SERVES 4

Prep + cooking time 30 minutes, plus cooling

For the rice

1 cup sushi rice

1 cup plus 2 tablespoons water

⅓ cup rice vinegar

2 tablespoons superfine sugar

½ teaspoon salt

2 nori sheets

1 teaspoon wasabi paste

2 long strips of cucumber, the length of the nori and about ½ inch thick

4 ounces smoked salmon

2 tablespoons pickled ginger

4 tablespoons soy sauce

1. Place the rice in a large bowl, cover it with cold water, and stir it, using your fingers. Repeat this two or three times until the water becomes clear.

2. Let the rice drain in a fine sieve for at least 30 minutes.

3. Place the rice and water in a small saucepan. Bring to a boil, lower the heat, cover, and cook for around 12 minutes. Take the pan off the heat and stand, covered, for 15 minutes.

4. Mix the rice vinegar, sugar, and salt in a bowl.

5. Spread the rice over a large flat plate, sprinkle with the vinegar mixture, and stir it in. If necessary, add more of the vinegar mixture. Cover with a clean, damp dish towel and let cool.

6. Take one nori sheet and place it on a bamboo mat with the longest side in line with your body and the ridged surface facing upward. With damp hands, cover three-quarters of the nori sheet with a thin layer of rice, leaving a band of nori at the top without rice.

7. Spread a little wasabi paste with your finger on top of the rice in a thin line, at the edge nearest to you. Then place a cucumber strip and some smoked salmon on top.

8. Use the bamboo mat to start rolling up the nori, tucking in the cucumber and salmon as you go. Once you have rolled up most of the nori, wet your finger and dampen the plain edge of nori. Finish rolling up the nori and the wet edge will stick the roll together. Repeat with the other nori sheet. Then, using a sharp knife, cut the rolls into eight even pieces.

9. Mix the remaining wasabi with the pickled ginger and soy sauce and serve alongside the nori rolls.

Shunned Fungus & Garlic Crostini

"The Shunned House" tells the tale of a "dingy, antiquated" house on Benefit Street in Providence, long abandoned, where people are said to have died "in alarmingly great numbers." The creepy setting was partly inspired by a real-life house in Providence, known to Lovecraft as the Babbit House, where his Aunt Lillian had once lived, although he was also inspired by another house he saw on a 1924 trip to Elizabeth, New Jersey, which he described in a letter to Lillian as "a hellish place where night-black deeds must have been done in the early seventeen-hundreds." He wrote "The Shunned House" soon after this trip. In the story, the narrator describes being fascinated with the house since his boyhood, and breaking into the cellar with his friends, noting: "We did not like the white fungous growths which occasionally sprang up in rainy summer weather from the hard earth floor," describing them as "truly horrible" and "detestable." Unusually for Lovecraft, who preferred to invent his own monsters, one of the possible explanations is the vampire legends of local folklore—"the dead who retain their bodily form and live on the blood or breath of the living." These tasty crostini celebrate fungus of a rather more delicious kind, along with a hefty dose of garlic to keep any bloodsuckers at bay.

Garlicky mushrooms, a sprinkling of fresh herbs, and crunchy toast combine in this delicious dish—ideal as a vegan hors d'oeuvre or a light meal. It's a great way to use up stale baguettes too.

SERVES 4

Prep + cooking time 20 minutes

2 thin baguettes
¼ cup olive oil
2 garlic cloves, 1 whole, 1 crushed
1 shallot, diced
4 ounces mixed wild mushrooms, chopped
1 tablespoon chopped parsley
black pepper

1. Cut the baguettes into slices diagonally, about 1 inch thick. Place the slices on a baking sheet and brush with 2 tablespoons of the olive oil.

2. Bake at 400°F for 4–5 minutes, until golden brown. Rub each slice with the whole garlic clove and keep the slices warm.

3. Heat the remaining oil in a skillet and sauté the shallot and crushed garlic for 3–4 minutes, then add the mushrooms and cook them until they have released all of their juices. Stir in the chopped parsley and season with pepper.

4. Spoon the mushroom mixture onto the crostini and serve.

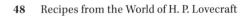

Howard's Potato Salad

While living in New York, Lovecraft became "exceeding fond" of a ten-cent potato salad served at an automat in Times Square. Years later, in 1936, perhaps missing this favorite meal, he included instructions for making his own in a letter to his Aunt Annie: "Both spuds & dressing were in fine condition, & I cut the former up to salad-size fragments, mixing them well with the mayonnaise & adding a sprinkling of sodium chloride. Finding the mayonnaise was a bit lacking in taste, I added a slight touch of catsup—which made an absolutely perfect & highly appetizing blend." If H.P.'s version doesn't appeal, try the recipe below instead—but don't forget the sodium chloride!

Hands down, potato salad is always the most popular salad at a barbecue or potluck. This one includes crisply cooked bacon so is packed with extra flavor. You could also swap in a large handful of crumbled blue cheese in place of the bacon and garnish with roughly chopped walnuts for extra crunch.

SERVES 4–6

Prep + cooking time 25 minutes, plus cooling

2 pounds new potatoes
4 ounces bacon
1 teaspoon vegetable oil
6 scallions
¾ cup mayonnaise
salt and black pepper

1. Halve the potatoes and cook in lightly salted boiling water until tender. Rinse under cold water and let cool.

2. Meanwhile, slice the bacon into thin strips. Heat the oil in a skillet and cook the bacon until golden; drain on paper towels and let cool. Finely slice the scallions, reserving some for garnish.

3. Put the potatoes, finely sliced scallions, and bacon in a large salad bowl. Gently stir in the mayonnaise. Season to taste with salt and pepper, garnish with the reserved scallions, and serve.

Weird Kales

*W*eird Tales was a pulp fiction and horror magazine that was first launched in 1923 and became one of the most prominent and regular publishers of Lovecraft's work— he was even offered the role of editor at one point, but declined as the idea of moving to Chicago, where the magazine was based, horrified him. Although he faced a few rejections that stung him badly, ultimately *Weird Tales* published no fewer than twenty-three of his works, some of them posthumously, making it an integral part of the Lovecraft story.

Here, kale gets a kick with the addition of red chili and lime juice. You could replace the kale with a small head of cabbage, and the dish also works well with collard greens. A delicious light meal in itself or, for a bigger meal, serve it alongside broiled chicken or steak.

SERVES 4

Prep + cooking time 25 minutes

1 tablespoon olive oil

1 garlic clove, crushed

1 large white onion, chopped

1 bunch (about 1 pound) curly kale, stems removed and leaves chopped

2 teaspoons lime juice

1 red chili, seeded and chopped

1 teaspoon salt

½ teaspoon black pepper

1. Heat the oil in a wok over medium heat. Add the garlic and onion and sauté for about 10 minutes or until the onion is translucent. Add the curly kale and stir-fry for an additional 5 minutes.

2. Stir in the lime juice and chili, season with salt and pepper to taste, and serve immediately.

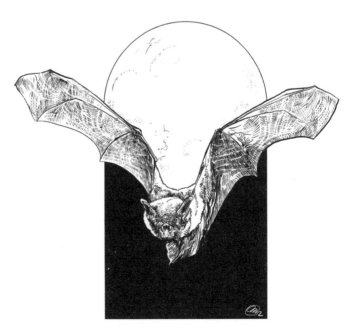

New England Rarebit

Lovecraft was a huge lover of cheese, and his letters reveal a fondness for the traditional Welsh rarebit, a meltingly tempting treat he describes as "magnificent" and something he would eat "with vast relish." Renamed in honor of his beloved New England, this classic comfort food will see you through many a scary story.

Grilled cheese but so much better, rarebit—also called rabbit—is a great choice whatever time of day. Serve with a crisp green salad to cut through the rich, melty cheese and shake over a little Worcestershire sauce for extra tang, if you like.

SERVES 4

Prep + cooking time 20 minutes

3½ tablespoons butter

⅓ cup all-purpose flour

1 cup strong beer

9 ounces mature cheddar cheese, grated

2 tablespoons whole-grain mustard

6 tablespoons caramelized onion or onion chutney

4 large slices of sourdough bread, lightly toasted on one side

salt and black pepper

1. Melt the butter in a small saucepan and stir in the flour. Cook for a few minutes, stirring constantly, then pour in the beer a little at a time, stirring until it forms a thick paste. Add the cheese, mustard, and season to taste. Cook for an additional 2 minutes until the cheese is melted and the mixture smooth. Remove from the heat.

2. Spread the chutney over the untoasted side of each piece of bread and then top with the cheese mixture, spreading it gently right to the edges.

3. Place under a medium–hot broiler for 4–6 minutes, or until the topping is melting and golden.

Coffin Loaf

Although Lovecraft's brand of horror was incredibly popular, sometimes his imagination was too much for some people. "In the Vault" tells the troubling tale of George Peck, an undertaker rather prone to cutting corners—he is described as "thoughtless, careless and liquorish." When Peck finds himself locked in a tomb, he realizes his only hope of escape is to pile up eight coffins and climb them to reach a small, high-up opening. As he climbs, though, the lid of the topmost coffin gives way and his feet fall into the decaying contents—and it seems that someone within isn't keen on letting Peck go. S. T. Joshi described "In the Vault" as a "commonplace tale of supernatrual vengeance," while in a 1925 letter to his Aunt Lillian, Lovecraft lamented that *Weird Tales* had "rejected [the story] on the ground (foolishly, I think), that its extreme gruesomeness would not pass Indiana censorship." Reading it does certainly require a strong stomach— hopefully the contents of this delicious stuffed loaf will be a bit more appetizing than those of Asaph Sawyer's casket . . .

A loaf of bread, hollowed out and stuffed to the brim with layers of delicious ingredients, this is not your average sandwich. Get creative and add whatever you fancy: roasted bell peppers, Parma ham or prosciutto, olive tapenade, pesto, cucumber . . . Make it up to 24 hours ahead to let the flavors mingle, if desired.

SERVES 6

Prep + cooking time 30 minutes

1 large round bread loaf

4 ounces salami

4 ounces sliced turkey

handful of basil leaves

3 tomatoes, sliced

5 ounces mozzarella cheese, drained and sliced

1 small red onion, cut into rings

2 handfuls of arugula

¾ cup pitted ripe black olives

3 ounces cheddar cheese or American cheese, thinly sliced

1. Cut the top off the loaf, about 1½ inches down from the top, and hollow out the inside of the loaf, pulling the soft bread out with your hands and leaving about a 1-inch edge.

2. Start by layering the salami into the bottom of the hollowed-out loaf, then cover with the turkey slices. Place a layer of basil leaves on top of the turkey, then layer with the tomato and mozzarella slices. Cover with the red onion rings and sprinkle with the arugula leaves. Top with the olives and finish with a layer of the cheese. Place the bread loaf top back on and press down firmly.

3. Wrap in wax paper and refrigerate until needed. Cut into wedges to serve.

Frightfully Frugal

Despite his long-lasting posthumous impact on the world of horror writing, Lovecraft's lack of commercial success in his own lifetime meant that he struggled financially and had to live a lifestyle that ranged from frugal to spartan. Lovecraft frequently went on economy kicks when money was tight, and went to great lengths to see how little he could spend. He wrote of coming across a decade-old can of cocoa in a cupboard, noting "it [has] deteriorated [and] acquired an earthy taste," but resolving to use it up anyway. When he was living in New York, he asked his aunts to send him his favorite Hershey's chocolate, explaining it was considerably cheaper to buy it in Rhode Island and ship it to him in the city.

In a 1932 letter to his friend, the writer Robert E. Howard, Lovecraft noted: "I have financial economy in eating worked out to a fine art, and know the self-service lunch rooms where I can get the best bargains. I never spend more than $3.00 per week on food, and often not even nearly that." It was rare for Lovecraft to describe a meal out to his aunts without also telling them how much it had cost, and in between "marvelously good & cheap dinner[s]" at "modest cafeteria[s]," he endeavored to live on canned foods, crackers, and other low-cost items, telling his Aunt Lillian in 1925: "with bread as a basis, I can certainly keep food down to 15c per day, except for a weekly spaghetti-meal at John's to break the monotony"—although in another letter he laments that "we went out to John's for dinner, where I had my usual meat-balls and spaghetti (raised from 30 to 35 cents, I mourn to say!)."

In another letter, he rejoices about having "found a restaurant which specializes in home-baked beans. It was closed on Sunday, but I shall try it some time soon. Beans, fifteen cents, with pork, twenty cents. With Frankfort [sic] sausages, twenty-five cents. Yes—here is a place which will replay investigation!"

Speaking of baked beans, they were probably one of his most consistently eaten foods, both when dining out and when eating at home, where he would

sometimes consume them cold (although he confided to Lillian that "beans & canned spaghetti are twice as good when hot"). In another letter, he told her:

. . . tonight I've begun my home dining program, having spent 30 cents for a lot of food which ought to last about 3 meals:

1 loaf bread ------------ 0.06
1 medium can beans ----- 0.14
½ lb. cheese ----------- 0.10
Total ----------------- 0.30

The beans I'll heat on the sterno, keeping the residue in a cup covered with a saucer. Yes—I'm getting to be a highly efficient housekeeper, & you can bet that any steep bills won't be in the direction of the larder!

Lillian may have expressed some concern about his diet, as his next letter says: "Bless my soul, but you-all mustn't be frightened at Grandpa's dietary program!! . . . All one really needs for a meal is some highly nutritious base, containing all the various food elements—proteids, vitamines, carbohydrates, &c.—in their proper balance—plus some tasty auxiliary to make it palatable—though of course it is all the better if the auxiliary itself can be of food value. In my case, the auxiliary does happen to be highly nourishing—being usually either baked beans or cheese or both."

Clearly, it would have been impossible to compile a book of recipes inspired by Lovecraft and not include baked beans—see page 60. He assures his aunt, however that "from time of time, I'll vary the 'meat course' by getting something instead of beans—canned spaghetti, beef stew, corned beef, &c. &c." Essentially, if it came in a can, it would do. If you decide to follow Lovecraft's lead, just make sure you emulate the characters from *At the Mountains of Madness*, and supplement your canned diet with a dash of lime juice—perfect for extra "vitamines."

Strange Feastings

In Lovecraft's short story "The Festival," the narrator tells us that "an old tradition of my father's had summoned me to strange feastings." This chapter is a selection of hearty dishes that could make up such a feast, each with its own special connection to the world of Lovecraft, from some of his personal top picks (including Sonia's Magical Spaghetti, page 75, and H.P.'s Favorite Boston Beans, page 60) to recipes inspired by his deliciously dark tales. Dagon's Paella (pages 67–69) honors the sinister fish-god of Innsmouth, while Spicy Night Gaunt Wings (page 80) allows you to have a taste of the terrifying flying creatures that haunted the young Howard's dreams. Each of the main courses in this chapter would make a perfect centerpiece at your next horrifying gathering, but a special mention must go to Cthulhu's Squid Spaghetti (page 70): pasta coated in a black, fishy sauce for a truly gothic experience.

"And what a classick repast! . . . But all things must end—& all stomachs have a limit of distensibility. I was askt if I had all I wanted, & I reply'd that I had all I could hold."

—*Letter from H. P. Lovecraft to Lillian D. Clark, November 29, 1924*

H.P.'s Favorite Boston Beans

Boston beans are a classic New England dish, and a confirmed favorite of Lovecraft's. He loved this dish for its heartiness as much as for its frugality, and wrote to his aunt of enjoying a meal of canned baked beans—a "unique delicacy"—with his friends Kleiner and McNeill, lamenting that a dash of "catsup" would have improved them, "but McNeill—simple soul—keeps none of these worldly, highly spiced devices in his primitive & ascetick larder." Try this delicious recipe for a warming, simple supper full of flavor.

If you don't have time to cook up a batch of Boston beans, try Lovecraft's recipe for beans on toast, described in a 1925 letter to his aunt: "Just you take a medium-sized loaf of bread, cut it into four equal parts, & add to each of these ¼ can (medium) Heinz beans & a goodly chunk of cheese. If the result isn't a full-sized, healthy day's quota of good fodder for an Old Gentleman, I'll resign from the League of Nations' dietary committee!"

A speedy twist on the classic dish, this recipe is vegetarian but you could add 4 ounces chunky bacon pieces at the same time as the celery and garlic. Great with cornbread, hot dogs, grilled cheese, or on hot, buttered toast. They also make a good side for the chicken wings on page 80.

SERVES 4

Prep + cooking time 40 minutes

2 tablespoons vegetable oil

1 large red onion, finely chopped

4 celery stalks, finely chopped

2 garlic cloves, crushed

1¾ cups canned diced tomatoes

1¼ cups vegetable stock

2 tablespoons dark soy sauce

2 tablespoons dark brown sugar

4 teaspoons Dijon mustard

3¼ cups canned mixed beans, drained and rinsed

¼ cup chopped parsley

1. Heat the oil in a heavy saucepan. Add the onion and cook over low heat for 5 minutes, or until softened. Add the celery and garlic and continue to cook for 1–2 minutes.

2. Add the tomatoes, stock, and soy sauce and bring to a boil, then reduce the heat to a fast simmer and cook for about 15 minutes, or until the sauce begins to thicken.

3. Add the sugar, mustard, and mixed beans and cook for an additional 5 minutes, or until the beans are heated through. Stir in the chopped parsley and serve.

Silver Key Chili Con Carne

Chili con carne was another favorite staple of Lovecraft's. He first came across it when watching his friend Kleiner eat it and he wrote to his aunts: "[it is] a highly spiced dish which I mean some day to investigate myself." Years later, he wrote: "I think this is becoming one of my favorite dishes."

His biographer, S. T. Joshi, describes him getting together with two friends, E. Hoffman Price and Harry Brobst, and concocting their own version, aiming to make it as spicy as they could: "the three behaved like mad scientists cooking up some nameless and sinister brew." Price collaborated with Lovecraft on more than just chili, however: the pair teamed up to write "Through the Gates of the Silver Key," a tale about Lovecraft's recurring character Randolph Carter. It was intended as a sequel to the earlier story "The Silver Key," a story Lovecraft wrote alone, but which intrigued Price so much he wanted to help continue the tale.

This is one to leave bubbling away low and slow to get the best flavor, and be generous with the toppings as they make all the difference. Great for a casual get-together, it can be made ahead and gently reheated, and quantities are easily upped for a crowd.

SERVES 4

Prep + cooking time
1 hour 15 minutes

2 tablespoons vegetable oil

2 onions, chopped

1 red bell pepper, seeded and cubed

2 garlic cloves, crushed

1 pound ground beef

1¾ cups beef stock

½–1 teaspoon chili powder

1¾ cups canned red kidney beans, drained

13-ounce can diced tomatoes

1 tablespoon tomato paste

1 teaspoon ground cumin

salt and black pepper

1¼ cups long-grain white rice

sour cream, dried red pepper flakes, grated cheddar cheese, and finely chopped scallions, to serve

1. Heat the oil in a saucepan over low heat. Add the onions and red pepper and gently fry, stirring now and then, for about 5 minutes until soft. Add the garlic and cook for another 1 minute until opaque.

2. Increase the heat slightly and add the meat. Fry until just brown, stirring and breaking up the meat with a wooden spoon. Pour in the stock, then add the chili powder, beans, tomatoes, tomato paste, cumin, and a dash of salt and pepper.

3. Bring to a boil, then cover, reduce the heat to as low as possible, and simmer very gently for 50-60 minutes, stirring occasionally so that it does not stick to the bottom of the pan.

4. Towards the end of the chili cooking time, cook the rice in lightly salted water, according to the package instructions, then drain.

5. Pile up the rice on four serving plates, dollop on the cooked chili, and top with sour cream. Sprinkle with chili flakes, grated cheddar, and scallions and serve immediately.

Jervas Dudley's Beef & Ale Casserole

The narrator of "The Tomb," Jervas Dudley, tells us how he one day stumbled upon an old tomb, "a half-hidden house of death," and found himself instantly drawn to it, returning over and over to try and gain entry. When he finally gains access, he begins to spend his nights exploring the tomb, but his parents notice a strange difference in him: his speech takes on eighteenth-century patterns and he sings an unusual song he has never heard before:

"Come hither, my lads, with your tankards of ale,
And drink to the present before it shall fail;
Pile each on your platter a mountain of beef,
For 'tis eating and drinking that bring us relief."

A sinister echo of times past—or a recipe for a delicious beef and ale casserole?

◆———————————————◆

". . . and here I would lie outstretched on the mossy ground, thinking strange thoughts and dreaming strange dreams."

◆———————————————◆

This hearty casserole improves with keeping, so tastes even better the day after it is made. Don't leave out the traditional Irish champ, flecked with scallions, which is ideal for mopping up the delicious gravy so none goes to waste. Choose floury potatoes, not waxy ones, to get the best creamy texture.

SERVES 5–6

Prep + cooking time 2 hours

2 tablespoons all-purpose flour

2 pounds braising steak, cut into chunks

2 tablespoons butter

1 tablespoon oil

2 onions, chopped

2 celery stalks, sliced

several thyme sprigs

2 bay leaves

1¾ cups English ale

1¼ cups beef stock

2 tablespoons molasses

1 pound parsnips, peeled and cut into wedges

salt and black pepper

For the champ

3 pounds potatoes, scrubbed

⅔ cup milk

3–4 scallions, finely chopped

¼ cup butter

1. Season the flour with salt and pepper and use to coat the beef. Melt the butter with the oil in a large, flameproof casserole and fry the beef in batches until deep brown. Drain with a slotted spoon while cooking the remainder.

2. Add the onions and celery and fry gently for 5 minutes. Return the beef to the pan and add the herbs, ale, stock, and molasses. Bring just to a boil, then reduce the heat and cover with a lid. Bake at 325°F for 1 hour.

3. Add the parsnips to the dish and return to the oven for an additional 30 minutes or until the beef and parsnips are tender.

4. Meanwhile, to make the champ, cook the potatoes in a large saucepan of salted boiling water for 20 minutes. Drain and peel away the skins, then return to the pan and mash. Beat in the milk, scallions, and butter. Season with salt and pepper and then serve with the casserole.

Kilderry Stew

Kilderry, a fictional, sleepy Irish village in County Meath, is Lovecraft's setting for his short story "The Moon-Bog." (Incidentally, County Meath is also the location of Dunsany Castle, home to Lord Dunsany, whom Lovecraft greatly admired—see page 140.) Described by S. T. Joshi and David E. Schultz as "one of the most conventionally supernatural" of Lovecraft's tales, "The Moon-Bog" is full of strange sounds in the night, unexplained "dancing lights," and whispered rumors. The narrator is warned that the place is "accursed," but like all good horror story protagonists, decides to go there anyway to visit his friend Denys Barry, who has just bought his ancestral home and is having it restored and draining the great bog—perhaps a reflection of Lovecraft's own reported desire to one day buy his family's ancestral home in England, a theme that also comes up in "The Rats in the Walls." Denys is warned by the locals about a local "preposterous legend" and suggestions of a guardian spirit who protects the bog. One night, the narrator sees strange dancers in the moonlight and hears odd, piping music as "white-clad bog-wraiths" take their revenge. This Irish stew should warm your bones after reading such a chilling tale.

Cooking slowly means that you can make the most of cheaper cuts of lamb in this warming winter one-pot recipe. For a simple, satisfying meal, add a loaf of crusty bread for soaking up that thick, flavor-packed gravy.

SERVES 4

Prep + cooking time 2¾ hours

2 tablespoons sunflower oil

2 pounds stewing lamb or lamb chops of different sizes

1 onion, roughly chopped

3 carrots, peeled and sliced

1¾ cups diced rutabaga

1¾ cups diced parsnips

2 tablespoons all-purpose flour

13 ounces potatoes, cut into chunks no bigger than 1½ inches square

3¼ cups lamb or chicken stock

3 sprigs of rosemary

salt and black pepper

4 tablespoons mixed chopped chives and rosemary, to garnish

1. Heat the oil in a large flameproof casserole, add the lamb, and fry until browned on both sides. Scoop out of the pan with a slotted spoon and transfer to a plate.

2. Add the onion to the pan and fry for 5 minutes, or until softened. Add the carrots, rutabaga, and parsnips and cook for 1–2 minutes, then stir in the flour. Add the potatoes, stock, rosemary, and plenty of salt and pepper and bring to a boil, stirring. Return the lamb to the pan, stir, and cover with a lid.

3. Turn the heat down to as low as possible and simmer gently for 2½ hours, stirring occasionally, or until the lamb is falling off the bones and the potatoes are tender.

4. Spoon into shallow bowls, removing the lamb bones, and sprinkle with the chopped chives and rosemary.

Dagon's Paella

Although Lovecraft himself seems not to have been a fan of seafood (in a 1921 letter to his mother, he describes "glid[ing] gracefully" over the oyster and fish courses at a dinner party "without consuming very much"), his fiction is packed with references to creatures of the deep, from Cthulhu to "the ancient Philistine legend of Dagon, the Fish-God."

Dagon first appears in the short story of the same name. After his ship is captured by Germans during World War I, a sailor manages to escape and finds himself adrift in a small boat, "drift[ing] aimlessly beneath the scorching sun . . . upon the heaving vastness of unbroken blue." He falls asleep, and wakens to find himself in a "slimy expanse of hellish black mire." He journeys forward through the mud, which gradually grows firmer. He scales a hill and finds himself looking out over a vast canyon where he finds a monolith inscribed with "aquatic symbols such as fishes, eels, octopi, crustaceans, molluscs, whales and the like," along with other beings that he assumes are the ancient gods of primitive fishing tribes.

Dagon also makes an appearance in "The Shadow over Innsmouth," when the curator of the local history society tells the narrator Olmstead about "a peculiar secret cult" known as the Esoteric Order of Dagon: the cult's popularity in Innsmouth is thought to be linked to the town's "sudden and permanent return of abundant fine fishing."

This paella features some of the aquatic creatures found carved on that unsettling monolith, but hopefully in a rather more appetizing fashion.

"I cannot think of the deep sea without shuddering at the nameless things that may at this very moment by crawling and floundering on its slimy bed, worshipping their ancient stone idols and carving their own detestable likenesses on submarine obelisks of water-soaked granite."

The popular Spanish signature dish paella has any number of variations and can include chicken and chorizo. This recipe keeps it deliciously simple with seafood only. Put the skillet in the center of the table so everyone can dig in, and place a bowl of lemon wedges alongside for squeezing over.

Continued overleaf →

SERVES 4

Prep + cooking time 55 minutes

2 tablespoons olive oil

1 large onion, finely diced

1 garlic clove, crushed

1 red bell pepper, cored, seeded, and
  chopped into ¼-inch dice

1½ cups paella rice

6 cups hot fish stock or water

pinch of saffron threads

2 large tomatoes, roughly chopped

10 ounces raw peeled jumbo shrimp

7 ounces clams, cleaned

7 ounces mussels, scrubbed and
  debearded

7 ounces squid, cleaned and cut into
  rings, tentacles discarded

1 cup frozen peas, thawed

2 tablespoons chopped parsley

salt and black pepper

1 lemon, cut into wedges, to serve

1. Heat the oil in a large skillet. Add the onion, garlic, and bell pepper to the pan and fry for a few minutes until they have started to soften, then add the rice and fry for 1 minute.

2. Pour enough hot stock over the rice to cover it by about ½ inch. Add the saffron threads and stir well. Bring the rice up to a boil, then add the tomatoes, and reduce the heat to a simmer. Stir well once again, then simmer for 10–12 minutes, stirring occasionally to prevent the rice from catching on the bottom of the pan.

3. Add the shrimp, clams, mussels (first discarding any that don't shut when tapped), and squid to the pan, along with a little more water or stock if the rice is too dry. Cook until the clams and mussels open (discarding any that don't), the shrimp are pink, and the squid turns white and loses its transparency.

4. Stir in the peas and parsley and cook for few more minutes until the peas are hot, then season to taste with salt and pepper.

Cthulhu's Squid Spaghetti

Cthulhu may have had the sort of looks that only a mother could love, but this monstrous deity has been a mainstay of the world of weird fiction since Lovecraft created it in the 1920s. Cthulhu is a cosmic being, but thanks to his octopus-like looks and submarine slumber, he will forever be associated with the sea, and is thought by some to have been inspired by Alfred, Lord Tennyson's poem "The Kraken," in which a monstrous creature sleeps an "ancient, dreamless, uninvaded sleep" in "the abysmal sea."

In this recipe, pair tentacled squid with a slick, black spaghetti for a tasty dose of cosmic horror.

Wow guests with a dramatic-looking bowl of contrasting black spaghetti, red chili, and green basil—it's super-simple to cook and looks amazing. Squid ink gives the spaghetti its gorgeous color and adds an extra dimension of subtle briny flavor.

SERVES 4

Prep + cook time 20 minutes

14 ounces black squid ink spaghetti

4 tablespoons olive oil, plus extra to serve

14 ounces prepared squid, cleaned and sliced into rings

4 garlic cloves, sliced

1 red chili, seeded if desired, and sliced

juice of 1 lemon

handful of basil leaves, chopped

salt and black pepper

1. Cook the pasta in a large saucepan of salted boiling water according to the package instructions until al dente.

2. Meanwhile, heat the oil in a large skillet. Pat the squid rings dry with paper towels, then add to the pan and cook over high heat for about 30 seconds until starting to brown. Add the garlic and chili and cook for a couple of seconds, taking care not to let the garlic burn. The squid should be white and just cooked through. Squeeze over the lemon juice and season with salt and pepper to taste.

3. Drain the pasta and return to the pan. Toss through the squid and basil, and add olive oil to taste. Serve immediately.

Innsmouth Lobster Tail

Although the creepy little seaside town of Innsmouth is best known for its weird frog-fish-human hybrid inhabitants (see page 20) and links to the cult of Dagon (see page 67), it also has a thriving fishing and lobstering industry—as the ticket-seller tells the narrator in a prolonged soliloquy on the town, it's "queer how the fish swarm right there and nowhere else." This decadent lobster dish makes the most of Innsmouth's weird and wonderful abundance.

When time is short but you deserve a little luxury, this is the recipe to turn to. It features tender chunks of lobster stirred through a heavenly creamy, spicy, sherry-laced sauce, and—best of all—it will be on the table in 20 minutes.

SERVES 4

Prep + cooking time 20 minutes

2 egg yolks, beaten

½ cup heavy cream

2 tablespoons butter

2 tablespoons dry sherry

½ teaspoon salt

1 tablespoon medium curry powder

¼ cup finely chopped cilantro leaves, plus extra leaves to garnish

1 pound cooked lobster tail meat, cut into bite-size pieces

To serve

lemon wedges

steamed rice

1. Beat together the egg yolks and heavy cream in a small bowl until well blended. Melt the butter in a saucepan over low heat, then stir in the egg mixture and sherry. Cook, stirring, for about 10–12 minutes or until the mixture thickens, but do not let boil.

2. Remove from the heat, then stir in the salt, curry powder, and cilantro. Stir in the lobster, then return the pan to low heat and cook gently until heated through.

3. Spoon into bowls, sprinkle with cilantro leaves, and serve with lemon wedges and steamed rice.

The Feast That Came to Sarnath

In "The Doom That Came to Sarnath," we learn of the ancient city of Ib, inhabited by strange-looking beings who were destroyed, along with their city, when men came to Mnar. After destroying Ib, the men built Sarnath, and "each year there was celebrated in Sarnath the feast of the destroying of Ib, at which time wine, song, dancing and merriment of every kind abounded." On the thousandth anniversary, the extravagant feast is "gorgeous beyond thought":

"There were eaten many strange delicacies at that feast; peacocks from the isles of Nariel in the Middle Ocean, young goats from the distant hills of Implan, heels of camels from the Bnazic desert, nuts and spices from Cydathrian groves . . . But most prized of all the viands were the great fishes from the lake, each of vast size and served upon golden platters with rubies and diamonds."

If you don't fancy devouring peacocks and camel heels, make a slightly more accessible version of the feast with this delicious whole trout baked with almonds. For extra Lovecraft points, serve on a jewel-studded platter. Enjoy it while you can; the Ib are coming . . .

Try this French classic for a quick and easy midweek meal for two. The buttery almonds provide a lovely foil for the delicate fish, and you could also use salmon. Serve with lemon or lime wedges and a green salad in summer and, in winter, steamed spinach alongside is perfect.

SERVES 2

Prep + cooking time 20 minutes

2 small whole trout, gutted and cleaned
¼ cup all-purpose flour, for dusting
¼ cup butter
3 tablespoons slivered almonds
salt and black pepper

1. Score the trout several times down each side. Season the flour with salt and pepper, and use to lightly dust the trout. Shake to remove any excess. Place in a shallow ovenproof dish.

2. Melt the butter and drizzle over the trout so that they are completely coated. Sprinkle with the almonds and bake at 375°F for about 15 minutes until cooked through. (Test by piercing a thick area of the fish with the tip of a knife—the flesh should flake easily.)

Sonia's Magical Spaghetti

S paghetti was one of Lovecraft's favorite foods, and he was particularly fond of his wife Sonia's version, which he mentions frequently in his letters to his aunts. The pair went out for "a fine spaghetti dinner" before they went to get their marriage license, and he describes her homemade spaghetti sauce as "inimitable, with meat prepared in magical ways beyond the divining of the layman." Despite this, Sonia taught him how to make it—he notes that his efforts were "a spectacular success." Here's hoping the version below would stand up to Lovecraft's incredibly high spaghetti standards.

Comforting, filling, and richly deep in flavor, this version of a quintessentially Italian recipe is bound to become a family favorite and is a great midweek standby. Serve it with plenty of grated Parmesan for sprinkling over.

SERVES 4

Prep + cooking time 30 minutes

8 pounds spaghetti

2 tablespoons olive oil

1 onion, finely chopped

2 garlic cloves, crushed

1 large carrot, peeled and finely chopped

1 cup coarsely chopped mushrooms

1 teaspoon dried oregano

½ teaspoon dried thyme

12 ounces ground round or ground sirloin beef

1¼ cups beef stock

1¼ cups tomato paste or tomato sauce

grated Parmesan cheese, to serve

1. Bring a large saucepan of lightly salted water to a boil, cook the spaghetti according to the package directions, then drain and keep warm.

2. Meanwhile, heat the oil in a large, heavy saucepan. Add the onion and cook over high heat for 2–3 minutes, then add the garlic, carrot, and mushrooms and cook for 5 minutes. Add the herbs and ground beef and cook for 10 minutes, until the meat is brown. Add the stock and tomato paste or sauce and continue to cook an additional 10 minutes, stirring occasionally, until the sauce has thickened and the meat and vegetables are tender and cooked through.

3. Add the spaghetti to the pan, mix with the meat and vegetables, and serve piled into serving bowls with the grated Parmesan on top.

Black Goat of the Woods Ravioli

In a 1924 letter to his Aunt Lillian, Lovecraft grandly informs her that he had his first taste of ravioli, which he later described to her as "meat encased in flat squares of pastry and smothered in tomato sauce and cheese." We've gone for a slightly different version here, made with pesto and goat cheese, inspired by one of Lovecraft's monstrous deities, Shub-Niggurath—also called the "Black Goat of the Woods with a Thousand Young." Shub-Niggurath's name is invoked in "The Whisperer in the Darkness," but she doesn't physically appear. However, she has become part of the Cthulhu Mythos over the years and has appeared in the works of many other authors.

In "The Whisperer in the Darkness," the narrator reads the transcript of a chilling recording:

> *". . . so from the wells of night to the gulfs of space, and from the gulfs of space to the wells of night, ever the praises of Great Cthulhu, of Tsathoggua, and of Him Who is not to be Named. Ever Their praises, and abundance to the Black Goat of the Woods. Iä! Shub-Niggurath! The Goat with a Thousand Young!"*

Dramatic stuff, and best enjoyed with a plateful of pasta.

Serve dinner in a dash by transforming store-bought ravioli into a something special by topping it with a speedy and delicious hazelnut and herb pesto. You can vary the herbs, depending on the season: basil is lovely in summer and, in winter, choose from parsley, sage, or thyme.

Continued overleaf →

SERVES 4

Prep + cooking time 20 minutes

2 tablespoons blanched hazelnuts

4 tablespoons chopped herbs, such as
  parsley, thyme, sage

1 cup arugula

1 small garlic clove, chopped

scant ½ cup extra-virgin olive oil

1 teaspoon lemon juice

2 tablespoons freshly grated hard goat
  cheese or Parmesan cheese, plus extra
  to serve

10 ounces fresh stuffed ravioli or
  tortellini

salt and black pepper

1. Place a dry skillet over a medium heat and toast
   the hazelnuts for 4–5 minutes, shaking the skillet
   frequently, until lightly golden. Transfer to a plate
   and set aside to cool.

2. Place the herbs, arugula, garlic, and cooled hazelnuts
   in a food processor and pulse briefly until coarsely
   chopped. With the motor running, add the olive oil
   in a steady stream and blend until almost smooth.

3. Scrape the pesto into a bowl, then stir in the lemon
   juice and grated cheese, and season to taste.

4. Cook the ravioli in a large pan of salted boiling
   water for 2–3 minutes, or according to the package
   instructions, until al dente. Drain and divide
   between four shallow bowls.

5. Drizzle with the pesto, then crumble or grate the
   extra cheese over the top to serve.

Ghoulash

Given his tendency to favor simple, hearty meals, it's no surprise that Lovecraft was a fan of goulash, which he described in a 1927 letter to his Aunt Lillian as follows: "Goulash is brazed [sic] beef covered with a highly seasoned sauce—a Hungarian dish very popular in restaurants, & a prodigious favorite of mine." This pork and paprika version is named after the ghouls of *The Dream-Quest of Unknown Kadath*, who help the protagonist Carter on his journey, although Carter has to disguise himself as a ghoul to blend in, shaving off his beard and "wallowing naked in the mould to get the correct surface, and loping in the usual slumping way, with his clothing carried in a bundle as if it were a choice morsel from a tomb." We're willing to wager this goulash will make a tastier morsel.

Paprika is the key ingredient in this Hungarian favorite, which is a great pick-me-up on a cold day. It freezes well and is easy to scale up so is a good choice for cooking in batches. Serve it on its own or over brown rice or buttered noodles.

SERVES 4

Prep + cooking time 30 minutes

2 tablespoons vegetable oil
1 pound pork tenderloin, cubed
1 onion, sliced
2 teaspoons smoked paprika
13-ounce can diced tomatoes
1 pound potatoes, diced
salt and black pepper
¼ cup sour cream, to serve
handful of chopped parsley, to garnish

1. Heat half the oil in a deep skillet. Add the pork, season to taste, and cook for 5 minutes, until browned all over. Remove from the skillet and set aside. Add the remaining oil to the skillet with the onion and cook for 5 minutes, until softened.

2. Stir in the paprika, then add the tomatoes and potatoes. Season to taste, bring to a boil, then reduce the heat and simmer for 10 minutes.

3. Return the pork to the skillet and cook for an additional 5 minutes, until the pork and potatoes are cooked through. Divide among serving bowls, top with the sour cream, and serve sprinkled with parsley.

Spicy Night-gaunt Wings

Among the many weird and spine-chilling creatures from *The Dream-Quest of Unknown Kadath*, the night-gaunts have to be the most unnerving. Described as "noxiously thin and horned and tailed and bat-winged," the night-gaunts capture Carter and carry him away, terrifying him with their alarming shapes and fondness for . . . tickling. As well as appearing in his fiction, these sinister creatures haunted Lovecraft's dreams as a child, with the young Howard plagued by nightmares in which the creatures carried him away.

We might not have any night-gaunts in the kitchen, but these chicken wings make a tasty substitute.

◆————————————————◆

". . . shocking and uncouth beings with smooth, oily, whale-like surfaces, unpleasant horns that curved inward toward each other, bat-wings whose beating made no sound, ugly prehensile paws, and barbed tails that lashed needlessly and disquietingly. And worst of all, they never spoke or laughed, and never smiled because they had no faces at all to smile with, but only a suggestive blankness where a face ought to be. All they ever did was clutch and fly and tickle; that was the way of night-gaunts."

◆————————————————◆

A must-make for your next barbecue. Ideally, marinate for two hours, but if you're short on time, even 30 minutes will help make them moist and tender. The heat will caramelize the sugars in the honey, adding a lovely crust. Not planning on a barbecue? These are great cooked under the broiler too.

Continued overleaf →

SERVES 4

Prep + cooking time 20 minutes,
plus marinating

8 large chicken wings
Italian parsley sprig, chopped, to garnish
lime wedges, to serve

For the marinade
1 garlic clove
2-inch piece of fresh ginger root, peeled
  and chopped
juice and finely grated zest of 2 limes
2 tablespoons light soy sauce
2 tablespoons peanut oil
2 teaspoons ground cinnamon
1 teaspoon ground turmeric
2 tablespoons honey
salt

For the yellow bell pepper dip
2 yellow bell peppers
2 tablespoons plain yogurt
1 tablespoon dark soy sauce
1 tablespoon chopped cilantro
black pepper

1. Place the marinade ingredients in a blender or food processor and blend until smooth.

2. Arrange the chicken wings in a shallow dish, pour the marinade over, and toss to cover. Cover and allow to marinate for 1–2 hours.

3. Soak eight bamboo skewers in cold water for 30 minutes.

4. Put the peppers for the dip on a hot barbecue or under a hot broiler for 10 minutes, turning occasionally, until they are charred and blistered. Remove and place in a plastic bag, then seal and leave until cool. Peel off the skins and remove the seeds and white membrane. Put the flesh into a food processor or blender with the yogurt and blend until smooth. Pour into a bowl, season with soy sauce and pepper to taste, and stir in the cilantro. Cover and chill until needed.

5. Remove the chicken from the marinade, thread onto the skewers, and cook on a hot barbecue or under a hot broiler for 4–5 minutes on each side, basting with the remaining marinade. Garnish with a parsley sprig, then serve with the dip and some lime wedges.

Cthulhu Tentacles

No doubt one of the best-known (and loved) of Lovecraft's creations, the terrifying creature Cthulhu has taken on a life of his own in the years since the writer dreamed him up, spawning spin-offs and games, and featuring in the works of many other authors. Cthulhu makes his first appearance in what is perhaps Lovecraft's most famous story, "The Call of Cthulhu," where the creature is described as "a monster of vaguely anthropoid outline, but with an octopus-like head whose face was a mass of feelers, a scaly, rubbery-looking body, prodigious claws on hind and fore feet, and long, narrow wings behind."

This crunchy calamari dish is a tentacled tribute to this most sinister of Lovecraft's Great Old Ones.

Served with a fragrant garlic and parsley dressing and a chunk of crusty bread to soak up the flavors, this is a pure taste of the Mediterranean. All you need to go with this simple but sublime dish are sunshine and a glass of something chilled.

Buy the prepared octopus and store it in the freezer for at least two days before you plan to cook it. This will ensure the meat is tenderized before you make the recipe.

Continued overleaf →

SERVES 4

Prep + cooking time 25 minutes

1 onion, cut into wedges
1 teaspoon whole cloves
8½ cups water
1 pound prepared octopus, frozen
6 tablespoons extra-virgin olive oil
2 garlic cloves, crushed
4 tablespoons chopped Italian parsley
1 teaspoon white wine vinegar
salt and pepper
crusty bread, to serve

1. Put the onion, cloves, and 1 tablespoon salt in a large saucepan and add the water. Bring to a boil.

2. Using tongs, dip the octopus in and out of the water about four times, returning the water to a boil before each dipping, then immerse the octopus completely in the water. (This helps to make the flesh tender.) If there are several pieces of octopus, dip them one at a time.

3. Reduce the heat and cook the octopus very gently for 1 hour, then check to see whether it's tender. Cook for an additional 15–30 minutes if necessary.

4. Allow it to cool in the liquid, then drain, cut into bite-size pieces, and place in a nonmetallic bowl.

5. Mix the oil with the garlic, parsley, vinegar, and salt and pepper to taste and add to the bowl. Mix well, cover, and chill for several hours or overnight.

6. Serve the octopus with crusty bread for mopping up the juices.

Baked Ark-ham

"Hoary and witch-accursed Arkham" ("Through the Gates of the Silver Key") is the fictional New England city where Lovecraft set many of his stories, including "Herbert West—Reanimator," "The Thing on the Doorstep," and many more. Enjoy this baked ham in honor of the imaginary town, made with ginger beer—a drink Lovecraft mentions several times in his letters.

You'll need to start this recipe the night before you want to serve it, to allow time for the ham to soak. If you can't find ginger marmalade, you could use the Bootleg Marmalade (page 21) or honey instead.

SERVES 10–12

Prep + cooking time 2½–3 hours, plus soaking

5½–8½ pound ham joint, either on the bone or boned and rolled

2 bay leaves

½ cup raw brown sugar

3 tablespoons ginger marmalade

⅔ cup ginger ale

1. Place the ham in a large saucepan of cold water and let soak for 2–12 hours, depending on the amount of salt in the cure (soak overnight if in doubt).

2. Drain the ham, then weigh it and calculate the cooking time based on 25 minutes per pound, plus 20 minutes. For a joint over 6½ pounds, allow 20 minutes per pound, plus 20 minutes. Return it to the pan and cover with fresh cold water. Add the bay leaves and 2 tablespoons of the sugar and bring to a boil. Cover, reduce the heat, and simmer for half the calculated cooking time.

3. Remove the ham from the water and strip off the skin. Stand the joint on a large sheet of aluminum foil in a roasting pan and score the fat diagonally in a trellis pattern. Mix the marmalade and remaining sugar and spread over the fat. Pour the ginger ale around the joint and enclose in the foil, sealing the edges firmly.

4. Bake at 375°F for the remaining cooking time. During cooking, baste the ham with the ginger ale, then rewrap in the foil. About 20 minutes before the end of the cooking time, fold back the foil, baste again, and return to the oven. Remove and let cool overnight.

Zoog Stroganoff

Early on in Randolph Carter's prolonged wanderings in *The Dream-Quest of Unknown Kadath* as he searches for the "marvellous city" of his dreams (see page 16), he passes through an enchanted wood. Although magical forests are often the setting for terrifying scenes in tales of horror, full as they are of dark shadows and wild creatures, this place is among the friendlier locations Carter travels through. It's home to "the furtive and secretive zoogs," a strange race of beings who live just over the border of the dream-world, but have been known to venture into the world of men. Lovecraft tells us: "Most of them live in burrows, but some inhabit the trunks of the great trees; and although they live mostly on fungi, it is muttered that they also have a slight taste for meat, either physical or spiritual, for certainly many dreamers have entered that wood who had not come out."

Fungus is a recurring theme in Lovecraft's fiction, perhaps because of its links to death and decay. As well as being the favored food of the zoogs, a strange fungal growth is seen in "The Shunned House" (see page 48), while some of Lovecraft's imagined creatures are even described as fungoid themselves. This delectable stroganoff features fungus in a slightly more appetizing form, and would surely be a hit with the zoogs—so why not try it yourself?

Enjoy dinner for two in double-quick time with this recipe that puts a speedy spin on the traditional beef stroganoff, smothering steaks in a wonderful sour cream and mushroom sauce. It's great served with either rice or pasta.

SERVES 2

Prep + cooking time 20 minutes

2 tablespoons butter

1½ tablespoons olive oil

2 shallots, finely chopped

2 cups sliced cremini mushrooms

2 teaspoons sweet paprika

⅔ cup sour cream

1 teaspoon rinsed and drained green peppercorns

2 sirloin steaks

1–2 tablespoons chopped parsley

salt and black pepper

steamed rice, to serve

1. Melt the butter in a skillet with 1 tablespoon of the oil and cook the shallots over a medium heat for 3–4 minutes, until softened. Add the mushrooms and fry for 3–4 minutes, until soft and golden.

2. Sprinkle in the paprika and heat for 1 minute, then stir in the sour cream and peppercorns. Season to taste and simmer for 2–3 minutes, until thickened slightly.

3. Meanwhile, heat the remaining oil in a large skillet and cook the steaks for 4–8 minutes, turning once, until done to your liking. Set aside to rest for 2–3 minutes, adding any juices to the stroganoff sauce.

4. Arrange the steaks on serving plates and serve with the sauce, parsley, and steamed rice.

R'lyeh Pie

In "The Call of Cthulhu," R'lyeh is the underwater city where Cthulhu and his horde lie in wait, trapped in dark vaults until "the stars [come] right again" and his cult can free him. Depicted as a "damp Cyclopean city of slimy green stone" and a "nightmare corpse-city," the descriptions of R'lyeh are almost as unsettling as those of Cthulhu himself. According to academic Dale A. Crowley, "Lovecraft uses the ocean and its black, unfathomable depths as a stand-in for the tombs, catacombs and underground hells in which we [usually] find his loathsome alien creatures." The sinister sunken city also has echoes of Atlantis, which Lovecraft referenced in several of his writings, but it lies beneath the waves of the Pacific Ocean, rather than the Atlantic, where Atlantis is said to be located.

This crispy spinach pie has all of the greenness of the city of R'lyeh, but hopefully none of the slime.

Using frozen spinach makes for fuss-free prep for this delicious Greek-style pie. All it needs alongside is a crisp green or tomato salad and perhaps a few steamed new potatoes. It is also lovely cold, so any left over can be enjoyed the next day.

Continued overleaf →

SERVES 4

Prep + cooking time 40 minutes

10 ounces frozen spinach

2 scallions, chopped

1 garlic clove, crushed

1⅓ cups crumbled feta cheese

2 eggs, beaten

pinch of grated nutmeg

2 tablespoons butter, melted

3 tablespoons olive oil

5 large phyllo pastry sheets

salt and black pepper

1. Place the spinach in a strainer, then pour over boiling water to thaw. Squeeze to remove excess water, then mix with the scallions, garlic, feta, and eggs. Add the nutmeg and season to taste.

2. Stir together the butter and oil and brush over the sides and bottom of an 8-inch springform cake pan. Unwrap the phyllo pastry and cover with damp paper towels until ready to use.

3. Working quickly, brush one sheet with the butter mixture and arrange in the pan, letting the excess pastry hang over the sides. Brush another sheet with the butter mixture, turn the pan a little, and arrange the pastry in the same way. Repeat the process until the bottom and sides of the pan are completely covered.

4. Spoon the filling into the pan, then fold the pastry edges in to cover the filling, scrunching them up a little as you work. Brush the top of the pie with a little more butter mixture and cook at 400°F for 20–25 minutes, until golden and crisp.

Keziah's Pumpkin Curry

In "The Dreams in the Witch House," Keziah Mason, the sinister witch, and her familiar, a huge rat with human hands called Brown Jenkin, appear to math student Walter Gilman in his dreams. A witch may, on first reading, seem like an unusual feature for a Lovecraftian tale, as he generally tends to favor alien or interdimensional beings. However, the story also incorporates elements that recur throughout Lovecraft's tales, including non-Euclidean geometry and quantum physics. Writer John Salonia suggests that what seem like very modern scientific concepts are here being presented as "science's first ironic stumbling steps towards rediscovering [the] ancient lore [of] Nyarlathotep." The line between magic and science is blurred, just as Lovecraft's writing so often blurs the line between horror and science fiction. In the story, Keziah, a "monstrous, leering old woman" (and, incidentally, one of only a handful of women featured in Lovecraft's stories) is seen holding a sacrificial knife and "a queerly proportioned pale metal bowl covered with curiously chased designs." The bowl is intended for collecting blood during a sacrificial ritual, but a far better use for it would be this suitably witchy pumpkin curry.

This fragrant, mild curry uses massaman curry paste, a spicy blend of gorgeous flavors that include cardamom and tangy lemongrass. If you can't get hold of Thai basil for the garnish, use mint instead. Steamed jasmine rice is the perfect accompaniment.

SERVES 4

Prep + cooking time 20 minutes

3-inch length of trimmed lemongrass stalk

1¾ pounds pumpkin or butternut squash, peeled and seeded

2 tablespoons vegetable oil

2 tablespoons Thai massaman curry paste

6 shallots, thinly sliced

6 green cardamom pods

2 teaspoons black mustard seeds

1 cup hot vegetable stock

14-ounce can coconut milk

juice of 1 lime, plus wedges to serve

small handful of Thai basil leaves and red chili slivers, to garnish

1. Finely chop the lemongrass stalk and dice the pumpkin into ½-inch cubes.

2. Heat the oil in a heavy saucepan, add the curry paste, shallots, lemongrass, cardamom, and mustard seeds, and cook over medium heat for 1–2 minutes, until fragrant.

3. Add the pumpkin and pour over the stock and coconut milk. Bring to a simmer, then cook for 10–12 minutes, or until the pumpkin is tender.

4. Remove from the heat and stir in the lime juice. Ladle into bowls, sprinkle with Thai basil and red chili slivers, and serve with lime wedges for squeezing over the curry.

Caseous Delicacies

"Cheese continues to be a staple of mine—just now we have some of that excellent Phoenix Swiss."

—*Letter from H. P. Lovecraft to Lillian D. Clark, July 6, 1925*

Alongside weird fiction and Providence, cheese was probably one of the great loves of Lovecraft's life, whether he was eating it on crackers, with donuts (see page 14), or sprinkled generously over his favorite meals.

He was incredulous at the notion that other people might not feel so fondly about it, declaring in one letter to his Aunt Lillian: "One might remark, however, that . . . belief in the indigestibility of cheese is the merest superstition; since most authorities—including him who ought to be Sir Charles Chaplin—agree that to the average stomach, cheese is both highly nutritious & properly digestible." To his friend Vernon Shea, he wrote in 1931: "How can anybody dislike cheese? And yet Little Belknap hates it as badly as you do! I don't suppose you would like spaghetti if you don't like cheese, for the two rather go together."

This was something of a recurring theme—to Lovecraft, spaghetti (and minestrone) meant cheese. In another letter to Lillian, he mused: "It's odd how superlatively fond I am of Italian dishes—though the omnipresence of my beloved CHEESE motif may go far toward accounting for it."

When it came to the type of cheese, however, he was characteristically particular. In a 1932 letter to Robert E. Howard, he explained that his preferred cheese would be "of the common hard variety, medium strength. I hate Roquefort, dislike cottage cheese, just tolerate Camembert and Brie, and am neutral about Limburger—which latter I've tasted only once." He also thought Swiss Gruyère "exquisite," and on a 1922 visit to New York he enthused to his aunts about a new cheesy discovery: "And oh, boy—the cheese!! The enclosed label represents a brand possessing absolutely unique virtues—mild, but with a flavor & individuality little short of the poetic! It comes in tinfoil'd triangles

pack'd in a flat circular box—a small box, but costing eighty cents! In this world, one usually gets what one pays for."

As ever, for Lovecraft, money was a problem; but cheese was one of the few areas where he wasn't prepared to scrimp. He wrote once of trying some "very strong cheese to economize on bulk," thinking that a stronger flavor would mean he needed to use less, but he disliked it, and quickly returned to his preferred dairy delights. Cheese was, he explained, "my favorite article of nourishment—&, I fear, my chief source of extravagance." For someone who economized so much, it's nice to know that he was willing to treat himself occasionally. For your own cheesy treat, try the New England Rarebit on page 52.

◆————————————————◆

"I was up at noon & wrote till evenings; then din[ed] on potato chips, bread, cheese & vanilla wafers."

—*Letter from H. P. Lovecraft to Lillian D. Clark, July 27, 1925*

◆————————————————◆

Toothsome
Sweets

"Last week I grew so fond of an ice cream diet that I often substituted a second plate [of ice cream] for a sandwich."

—*Letter from H. P. Lovecraft to Lillian D. Clark, June 16, 1931 (dated 1781)*

Lovecraft is known for having something of a sweet tooth: in a 1936 letter to Mrs. Fritz Leiber, he told her: "my tastes call for . . . desserts as close to 100% $C_{12}H_{22}O_{11}$* as possible." We've already seen that he thought a donut made a perfectly suitable breakfast, but there's a wealth of sugary treats in this chapter that make the most of all Lovecraft's favorite flavors—and our best-loved stories. Enjoy the alarmingly wobbly Panna Cotta from Beyond (page 104), or satisfy your sugar (and horror) cravings with the Meringues of Madness Pie (pages 116–118). There are also a couple of delicacies inspired by Lovecraft's beloved Kalem Club, the group of writers with whom he spent many happy hours in New York, eating, drinking, and sharing ideas: try the Kalem Club Coffee Cake (pages 119–121) or Kleiner's Crumb Cake (page 114). And, of course, we've indulged Lovecraft's fondness for ice cream, too, with a tasty coffee-flavored zabaglione (page 130) and a truly decadent chocolate sundae.

---

* That's sucrose, or table sugar, to the less scientifically minded among us.

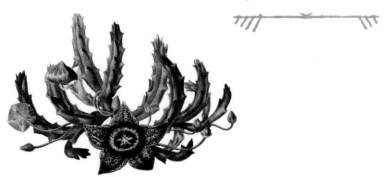

Donut Bholes

Among Lovecraft's many weird and alarming creatures are the bholes (sometimes spelled dholes). The first time we hear of them, in *The Dream-Quest of Unknown Kadath*, we are told, "no one has ever seen a bhole or even guessed what such a thing may be like," and "they cannot be seen because they creep only in the dark." In the later story "Through the Gates of the Silver Key," the hero Carter sees the ground "festering with gigantic bholes." These giant wormlike creatures are several hundred feet long and unpleasantly slimy. This churro-esque tribute to them is a little more appetizing—we think you'll agree.

These are best eaten on the day they are made. For an extra-indulgent treat, serve them with a homemade chocolate-maple dipping sauce: just melt ¾ cup chopped bittersweet chocolate, 3½ tablespoons unsalted butter, and 1 tablespoon maple syrup together, stirring well.

MAKES 12

Prep + cooking time 30 minutes

1¾ cups all-purpose flour
¼ teaspoon salt
5 tablespoons superfine sugar
1¼ cups water
1 egg, beaten
1 egg yolk
1 teaspoon vanilla extract
4 cups sunflower oil
1 teaspoon ground cinnamon

1. Mix the flour, salt, and 1 tablespoon of the sugar in a bowl. Pour the water into a saucepan and bring to a boil. Take off the heat, add the flour mixture, and beat well. Then return to the heat and stir until it forms a smooth ball that leaves the sides of the pan almost clean. Remove from the heat and allow to cool for 10 minutes.

2. Gradually beat the whole egg, egg yolk, then the vanilla into the flour mixture until smooth. Spoon into a large nylon piping bag fitted with a ½-inch-wide plain tip.

3. Pour the oil into a medium saucepan to a depth of 1 inch. Heat to 340°F on a candy thermometer, or pipe a tiny amount of the mixture into the oil. If the oil bubbles instantly, it is ready to use. Pipe coils, S-shapes, and squiggly lines into the oil, in small batches, cutting the ends off with kitchen scissors. Cook the bholes for 2–3 minutes until they float and are golden, turning over if needed to brown evenly.

4. Using a strainer spoon, lift the bholes out of the oil, drain well on paper towels, then sprinkle with the remaining sugar mixed with the cinnamon. Continue piping and frying until all the mixture has been used. Serve warm or cold.

Curwen's Spiced Cookies

Joseph Curwen, the apparently ageless wizard and merchant who appears in *The Case of Charles Dexter Ward,* is described as an "outcast, suspected of vague horrors and daemonic alliances." Despite this, he has "a virtual monopoly on the town's shipping trade in saltpetre, black pepper and cinnamon." Over a century after Curwen's murder, his descendant Charles Dexter Ward begins investigating his family history, and in Curwen's books comes across a method for resurrecting the dead using their "essential saltes." Rather than tinkering with his sinister ancestor's necromancy recipes, perhaps Charles should have used some of Curwen's trading spices to make these tasty cookies instead. No essential saltes required.

Fill your kitchen with the amazing aroma of cinnamon, clove, and cardamom as you bake these wonderful cookies. Full of festive flavors, they'd make a lovely Christmas gift piled into a jar with a jaunty plaid ribbon tied around it.

MAKES 30–40

Prep + cooking time 30 minutes

1½ sticks unsalted butter, softened

1 cup firmly packed dark brown sugar

1 extra-large egg, lightly beaten

½ teaspoon ground cinnamon

¼ teaspoon ground cardamom

¼ teaspoon ground cloves

2⅔ cups all-purpose flour, plus extra for dusting

1 teaspoon baking powder

½ teaspoon salt

1. Line three baking sheets with nonstick baking parchment. Place the butter and sugar in a large bowl and beat together with a handheld electric mixer until light and fluffy. Add the egg and spices and beat well. Stir in the flour, baking powder, and salt and mix until combined.

2. Turn the dough out onto a floured surface and knead lightly until smooth. Roll out to ⅛ inch thick, then cut out 30–40 shapes, such as stars, or stamp out circles using a 2½-inch fluted cutter.

3. Place the cookies on the prepared baking sheets and bake at 350°F for 14–16 minutes, until lightly golden and tinged brown around the edges. Transfer to wire racks to cool.

Lucullus Languish's Mince Pies

Although he is best known for his weird fiction, Lovecraft also occasionally dabbled in poetry, and one of his longest (and strangest) poetic offerings was "The Poet's Nightmare." In it, a young poet named Lucullus Languish, "student of the skies / And connoisseur of rarebits and mince pies," overdoes it on the sweet stuff, consuming all his favorites (including "a monstrous lot of cake") and finding himself transported in his sleep to a nightmarish hellscape beyond the reaches of space and time. So while it's probably wise to heed Lovecraft's warning and not overindulge with these mince pies, we're sure one or two won't hurt.

Mincemeat is a much-loved feature of English Christmas celebrations as a filling for traditional mince pies. Despite its name, it's a sweet pie filling made with chopped dried fruit and spices. The name comes about as, centuries ago, it did contain meat. You can find mincemeat in specialty stores and online. This recipe gives a deliciously fresh way of using it.

SERVES 6

Prep + cooking time 1 hour, plus chilling

⅔ cup all-purpose flour, plus extra for dusting

⅔ cup whole-wheat flour

6 tablespoons chilled butter, diced

½ cup ground almonds (almond meal)

2 tablespoons superfine sugar

grated zest of 1 orange

1 egg, beaten

1¼ cups mincemeat

3 clementines, segmented

milk, to glaze

confectioners' sugar, for dusting

1. Put both the flours in a bowl, add the butter, and rub in with your fingertips until the mixture resembles fine bread crumbs. Stir in the almonds, sugar, and orange zest, then add the egg and mix to a firm dough.

2. Knead the dough briefly on a lightly floured surface, then roll out and use to line a 9-inch loose-bottom fluted tart pan. Prick the bottom with a fork, chill for 15 minutes, then line with nonstick parchment paper and add pie weights or dried beans. Bake at 375°F for 10–15 minutes. Remove the paper and weights or beans and return to the oven for an additional 5 minutes.

3. Mix the mincemeat and clementine segments, then fill the pie shell. Gather up the dough trimmings, reroll, and cut into differently sized stars. Place on the topping, brush with milk, and dust with confectioners' sugar.

4. Bake at 375°F for 18–20 minutes until the fruit is caramelized and the stars look baked. Dust with confectioners' sugar and serve warm or cold.

"To bless the just, or cast a warning spell
On those who dine not wisely, but too well."

Panna Cotta from Beyond

In Lovecraft's short story "From Beyond," the narrator visits a scientist friend, Crawford Tillinghast, who has created an "accursed electrical machine" that he claims can enable people to perceive things beyond the five senses. As Tillinghast gleefully demonstrates his device, the narrator describes seeing "great, inky, jellyish monstrosities which flabbily quivered in harmony with the vibrations from the machine." The true horror in this story lies not so much in the things themselves as in the fact that they are there all the time, "float[ing] and flop[ping] about you and through you every moment of your life," but until now it had not been possible to perceive them. This story is perhaps the most blatant example of a recurring theme throughout Lovecraft's work, described by academic Peter Dendle: that "the malign beings of the primal past, and of the furthest reaches of space, are not so distant as the human observer might wish."

These delectable little panna cottas have a bit of a quiver to them, but are more scrumptious morsels than otherworldly monstrosities.

An elegant, make-ahead option for a stress-free finale to a special dinner. For a coffee version of this delicate dessert, substitute 2 teaspoons of strong coffee for the passion fruit and decorate each one with chocolate coffee beans.

SERVES 4

Prep time 20 minutes, plus setting

2 gelatin sheets
8 passion fruit
¾ cup sour cream
½ cup plain yogurt
1 teaspoon superfine sugar
vanilla bean, split

1. Soften the gelatin sheets in cold water. Halve the passion fruit and remove the seeds, working over a bowl to catch as much juice as you can. Reserve the seeds for decoration.

2. Combine the sour cream, yogurt, and passion fruit juice.

3. Put ¼ cup water in a small saucepan, add the sugar and the seeds from the vanilla bean, and heat gently, stirring until the sugar has dissolved. Drain the gelatin and add to the pan. Stir until dissolved, then allow to cool to room temperature.

4. Mix the gelatin mixture into the sour cream, then pour into four ramekins or molds. Refrigerate for six hours or until set.

5. Turn the panna cotta out of their molds by briefly immersing each ramekin in very hot water. Spoon over the reserved passion fruit seeds to decorate.

Iranon's Fruit & Berry Pie

The Quest of Iranon" is one of Lovecraft's Dunsanian tales (see page 140), and is often marked out for its particularly flowery language. It sees Iranon, a youth wearing a crown of vines, arrive at the granite city of Teloth, singing songs and telling the inhabitants of his quest to rediscover his home city of Aira, from where he was exiled as a young child. This desire to return to a city once visited and now lost to the protagonist is a theme that comes up in several of Lovecraft's tales, perhaps most notably *The Dream-Quest of Unknown Kadath*. Iranon pairs up with a local boy, Romnod, and they search for Aira together. The wanderers eat "plentifully of fruit and red berries" on their journey, and eventually reach a city called Oonai, where they settle for a time. As Romnod grows old (and a little too fond of wine), Iranon retains his youthful beauty, and eventually sets out once more in search of Aira, but makes a devastating discovery about his longed-for hometown.

The story's poignant ending may leave a bitter taste, so we suggest you sweeten things with this rustic fruit pie, made with the fruits on which Iranon and Romnod dined during their travels.

The great thing about this charmingly rustic-looking pie is that you don't have to worry about any fiddly fitting the pie dough into a pan—simply pile up the fruit filling in the middle and shape the dough up around it. Serve it warm with plenty of vanilla ice cream or custard for dessert heaven.

Continued overleaf →

SERVES 6

Prep + cooking time 1 hour,
plus chilling

2¼ cups all-purpose flour, plus extra
for dusting

¾ cup confectioners' sugar

½ cup unsalted butter, at room
temperature, diced

2 eggs

a little milk or beaten egg, to glaze

superfine sugar, to decorate

For the filling

2 cooking apples (about 1 pound), cored,
peeled, and thickly sliced

1¼ cups frozen mixed berries (no need
to thaw)

½ cup confectioners' sugar

2 teaspoons cornstarch

1. Put the flour on a large board or straight onto the work surface, add the confectioners' sugar and butter, then make a dip in the center and add the eggs. Begin to mix the eggs and butter together with your fingertips, gradually drawing the flour and sugar into the mix until it begins to clump together and you can squeeze the dough into a ball. Knead the dough lightly, then chill in the refrigerator for 15 minutes.

2. Mix together the apples, frozen mixed berries, confectioners' sugar, and cornstarch for the filling.

3. Grease a large baking sheet. Roll out the dough on a lightly floured surface until it forms a rough-shaped circle about 13 inches in diameter. Lift it over a rolling pin onto the prepared baking sheet. Pile the fruit mix high in the center of the dough, then bring the edges of the dough up and around the fruit, shaping into soft pleats and leaving the center of the fruit mound exposed.

4. Brush the outside of the pie with a little milk or beaten egg and sprinkle with superfine sugar. Bake at 375°F for 20–25 minutes, until the pie is golden and the fruit tender.

Meteor Cakes

"The Colour Out of Space," which S. T. Joshi describes as "Lovecraft's greatest triumph in the depiction of an extraterrestrial entity," deals with the after-effects of a meteor striking farmland on the outskirts of Arkham. The rock, a "stony messenger from the stars," which Lovecraft describes as "oddly soft," changes in size and is slightly luminous, with a color that is impossible to describe. In line with Lovecraft's move toward science fiction over supernatural horror, the rock is investigated by scientists from Miskatonic University, but they are unable to ascertain what it is, and this is where Joshi and David E. Schultz hold that the horror in the story is found: we do not know whether the rock itself is animate, whether it acted as a vessel for animate entities, or where it came from. We'll look at the strike's impacts on page 112, but this recipe is all about the space rock itself. These drop scones—or, in this instance, meteor cakes—resemble the rocky texture of the space boulders, but are little tastier!

Light and fruity, these are a lovely treat with a cup of tea or coffee. They are best eaten on the day they are made and are particularly good still warm from the oven. For best results, don't be tempted to add too much milk: the dough should be thick and lumpy.

MAKES 10–12

Prep + cooking time 30 minutes

2 cups all-purpose flour

4½ teaspoons baking powder

1 teaspoon ground cinnamon

½ teaspoon ground ginger

1 stick unsalted butter, softened

½ cup raw sugar, plus extra for sprinkling (optional)

1 teaspoon grated orange zest

⅔ cup golden raisins

½ cup dried currants

¼ cup mixed peel or chopped candied cherries

1 extra-large egg, lightly beaten

3–4 tablespoons milk

1. Line a large baking sheet with nonstick baking parchment. Sift the flour, baking powder, and spices into a large bowl. Add the butter and rub in with the fingertips until the mixture resembles fine bread crumbs, then stir in the sugar, orange zest, golden raisins, currants, and mixed peel or cherries. Pour in the egg, adding enough of the milk to form a soft, slightly sticky batter.

2. Drop 10–12 mounds of the batter onto the prepared baking sheet, so that they resemble rocks, and sprinkle with a little extra sugar, if using.

3. Bake at 400°F for 18–20 minutes, until golden. Transfer to a cooling rack to cool slightly, then serve warm.

King Kuranes's Cornish Cream Tea

During the many weird wanderings that make up *The Dream-Quest of Unknown Kadath*, our hero Carter pays a visit to his old friend King Kuranes, who has lived in the dream-lands for so long that his body in the waking world is dead. Full of nostalgia for his childhood, Kuranes has tried to re-create it by building "a little Cornish fishing village with steep cobbled ways," where the inhabitants are taught to speak "as best [they] could in the quaint tones of far Cornwall." It seems clear that the king would have been a fan of that most Cornish of treats, the traditional cream tea. Just make sure you prepare it in true Cornish fashion: jam first, then cream.

Eat these delicious English scones the authentic Cornish way: still warm from the oven and with the preserves or jam spread on first, and then the cream, never the other way around! In Cornwall, these are served with clotted cream, which can be hard to find, so you can substitute whipped cream.

MAKES 10

Prep + cooking time 30 minutes

1¾ cups all-purpose flour, plus extra for dusting

2½ teaspoons baking powder

3 tablespoons salted butter, chilled and diced

2 tablespoons superfine or granulated sugar

½ cup milk, plus extra to glaze

To serve

strawberry jam or preserves

whipped cream or clotted cream (see above)

1. Sift the flour and baking powder into a bowl or food processor. Add the butter and rub in with the fingertips or process until the mixture resembles fine bread crumbs. Add the sugar and milk, reserving 2 tablespoons of milk, and mix or blend briefly to a soft, slightly sticky dough. Add the reserved milk if the dough feels dry.

2. Knead the dough lightly on a lightly floured surface until smooth, then roll out to ¾ inch thick. Cut out 10 circles, using a 2-inch plain cookie cutter, rerolling the trimmings to make more. Place slightly apart on a greased baking sheet and brush with milk.

3. Bake at 425°F for 12 minutes, until well risen and golden. Transfer to a wire rack to cool.

4. Halve the scones and serve topped with jam and cream.

Colour Out of Space Crumble

If you've already devoured your own Meteor Cakes (page 108), it may be time to explore the repercussions of the meteor strike described in "The Colour Out of Space."

It's not just the fruit that seems to have been affected by the meteor; a low mood grips the farm's inhabitants, and they notice that the anatomy of the area's wild animals is "not quite right." The following spring, the orchard blooms in strange colors with a "haunting familiarity," but by the fall, all the vegetation in the area is "fast crumbling to a greyish powder." S. T. Joshi and David E. Schultz describe the story as "the first of [Lovecraft's] major tales to effect the union of horror and science fiction that became the hallmark of his later work." The science fiction aspects of the meteor strike and the resulting scientific investigation contrast with the chilling descriptions of the crumbling landscape and the pervading sense of unease. The farmer's wife, Gabby, seems to go mad and is locked away in an upstairs room, mirroring the classic gothic trope of "the mad woman in the attic" seen in works such as Charlotte Brontë's *Jane Eyre* and Charlotte Perkins Gilman's "The Yellow Wallpaper"; Joshi and Schultz suggest that Gabby's visions could be seen to echo those suffered by Lovecraft's own mother during her illness. Either way, the impact is harrowing.

This crumble, made with apples and pears like those once grown by the farmers before the strange space rock poisoned their land, is sweet and moreish—without a hint of "sickishness."

This is a great option for a cold winter's evening after a tiring day, when you crave something sweet, warming, and comforting. Divide it into bowls, top with custard or whipped cream, and then curl up on the couch and dig in.

SERVES 4

Prep + cooking time 30 minutes

3 x 4-ounce containers diced apple pieces in juice

15-ounce can pear slices in juice

½ cup applesauce

½ cup ground almonds (almond meal) or ground hazelnuts

½ cup chopped mixed nuts

2 cups fresh bread crumbs

¼ cup granulated sugar

1 teaspoon ground cinnamon or allspice

4 tablespoons butter, melted

1. Mix the apples and pears with the applesauce and transfer to an ovenproof dish.

2. Mix the ground and chopped nuts with the bread crumbs, sugar, and spices. Mix in the melted butter until well coated, then spoon the mixture over the fruit. Bake at 400°F for 20–25 minutes, until crunchy and golden.

Kleiner's Crumb Cake

Rheinhart Kleiner, Lovecraft's good friend and member of the Kalem Club (see page 119), was a huge fan of crumb cake, and Lovecraft made a point of buying it when it was his turn to host one of their evenings together. Unfortunately, Kleiner didn't show up, leading Lovecraft to lament in a letter: "The amount of crumb-cake remaining is prodigious . . . I can see my meals mapped out for me for two days!! Ironic circumstance—I got the crumb-cake especially for Kleiner, who adores it, & in the end he was absent; so that I, who don't particularly care for it at all, must swallow unending quantities in the interests of economy!" Perhaps if Howard had had this recipe, he would have enjoyed it a little more. If you make it for pals, make sure they're actually coming before you start baking.

This simple cake, made even easier by using ready-baked cake, is a twist on the classic crumb cake. Served cold, it makes a lovely teatime treat, but can also be dressed up as a dessert, served warm with cream or mascarpone.

SERVES 6

Prep + cooking time 30 minutes

1¼ sticks unsalted butter, softened, plus extra for greasing

⅔ cup granulated sugar

¾ cup all-purpose flour, sifted

2 teaspoons baking powder

½ cup ground hazelnuts

2 extra-large eggs, lightly beaten

2 teaspoons finely grated orange zest, plus extra to decorate

1 teaspoon orange extract

For the crumb topping

4-ounce store-bought plain yellow cake or pound cake

½ cup ground hazelnuts

4 tablespoons unsalted butter, melted

1. Grease a 9-inch square cake pan and line with nonstick baking parchment.

2. Break the cake into pieces in a bowl and crumble with your fingers until it resembles bread crumbs, then mix together with the ground hazelnuts and melted butter.

3. In a separate large bowl, place all of the cake ingredients and beat together with a handheld electric mixer until pale and creamy. Spoon the batter into the prepared pan and sprinkle with the crumb topping mix.

4. Bake at 400°F for 22 minutes, or until golden and firm to the touch. Turn out of the pan onto a wire rack and peel away the lining paper.

5. Serve warm or cold, decorated with orange zest.

Meringues of Madness Pie

Lovecraft's epic adventure *At the Mountains of Madness* was inspired by the writer's lifelong fascination with Antarctica—he had been writing about the area since he was a boy. Lovecraft expert John M. Navroth suggests that the story "can be considered Lovecraft's literary avatar of a deliberate shift from supernaturalism to 'rational' science," which can be seen in the detailed scientific description of the dissection of the Old Ones (see page 45). At the time, much of Antarctica remained unexplored—the first successful expedition to the South Pole had taken place just twenty years earlier—and the region's chilling remoteness made it the perfect setting for this tale, as Lovecraft could position his terrifying ancient city directly within the real world, albeit a part of it nobody had ever been to before. Lovecraft's explorers discover a "titanic mountain rampart" made up of peaks higher than any others previously seen on Earth, with "witch-like cones and pinnacles" and "stark nightmare spires." Take inspiration from these monstrous mountains and whip up a meringue to emulate their snowy peaks.

A showstopping creation that combines a light-as-a-feather cake base, an ice-cold berry filling, and warm toasted meringue. A real treat for any summer celebration, this spin on the retro favorite baked Alaska is utterly irresistible.

Continued overleaf →

SERVES 6

Prep + cooking time 45 minutes,
plus cooling and chilling

For the cake base

4 eggs

½ cup superfine sugar

¾ cup all-purpose flour

finely grated zest and juice of 1 lemon

For the filling and topping

13 ounces frozen fruit

1¼ cups mascarpone

1 teaspoon vanilla bean paste

2 tablespoons confectioners' sugar

3 tablespoons crème de cassis or
   cranberry juice

3 large egg whites

¾ cup superfine sugar

red currants or other berries, to decorate
   (optional)

1. Grease and flour a 10-inch pie pan.

2. To make the cake, whisk the eggs and sugar in a large bowl until very thick and the mixture leaves a trail when lifted. Sift the flour in over the surface and fold in very gently. Add the lemon zest and juice and fold in until just mixed. Pour the mixture into the prepared pan, tilting the pan to ease it into an even layer.

3. Bake at 350°F for 12–15 minutes until the top of the cake is golden and the center springs back when lightly pressed. Cool the cake in the pan for 5–10 minutes, then carefully turn it out onto a wire rack and allow to cool completely.

4. Line a baking sheet with nonstick baking parchment.

5. Place the frozen fruit in a bowl or food processor with the mascarpone, vanilla paste, confectioners' sugar, and crème de cassis or cranberry juice. Beat or pulse until very thick and smooth.

6. Spread the fruit mixture over the cake base in a thick, even layer. Place on the prepared baking sheet, then cover loosely with plastic wrap and chill in the freezer for about 15 minutes.

7. Meanwhile, make the meringue mixture by whisking the egg whites until they form soft peaks. Gradually add the superfine sugar, a spoonful at a time, whisking well between each addition, until the meringue is thick, glossy, and forms stiff peaks.

8. Spoon the meringue mixture over the filling, using the back of the spoon to create peaks. Slide under a hot broiler for 1–2 minutes, until the top is beginning to color nicely.

9. Cut into wedges, decorate with red currants or other berries, if you desire, and serve immediately.

Kalem Club Coffee Cake

While he was living in New York, Lovecraft became part of a tight-knit group of friends who have become known as the Kalem Club, supposedly because most of their surnames began with K, L, or M: members included Rheinhart Kleiner, Everett McNeill, Frank Belknap Long, George Kirk, Arthur Leeds, and, of course, Lovecraft himself. Lovecraft usually refers to this group as "the Boys" in his letters, which are full of references to the long evenings they spent together, drinking coffee and talking into the small hours, or sometimes all night. The friends took it in turns to play host, and Lovecraft enjoyed the role, taking great care to ensure he had adequate refreshments to offer his guests. In a 1925 letter to his Aunt Lillian, he wrote: "I lately learned from Sonny that honest old McNeill feels hurt because some of the members do not serve coffee, despite his own conscientious preparation of the stuff when he is host; hence have decided to humour him this once." Unfortunately, Howard admitted he "[couldn't] make the darned stuff," so he went out and bought "a splendid aluminum pail or milk can with a handle . . . to use in going out for hot coffee." If you feel so inclined, you can head out with a bucket to buy the coffee for this cake from your local barista; but even if you just use instant, this coffee cake is sure to satisfy at your next literary salon.

Baking doesn't get much easier than this: simply add all the ingredients at once, mix, and bake for a perfectly moist and tasty coffee cake. It can be stored in an airtight container for up to three days in a cool place.

Continued overleaf →

SERVES 8

Prep + cooking time 50 minutes

¾ cup butter, softened

¾ cup light brown or superfine sugar

1½ cups self-rising flour

1 teaspoon baking powder

3 eggs

3 teaspoons instant coffee, dissolved in 2 teaspoons boiling water

For the frosting

⅓ cup butter, at room temperature

1⅓ cups confectioners' sugar, sifted

3 teaspoons instant coffee, dissolved in 2 teaspoons boiling water

2 ounces semisweet chocolate, melted

1. Beat all of the cake ingredients in a mixing bowl or a food processor until smooth.

2. Divide the mixture evenly between two 7-inch cake pans, greased and bases lined with oiled waxed paper, and spread the surfaces level. Bake at 350°F for 20 minutes until well risen, the cakes are browned and spring back when gently pressed with a fingertip.

3. Leave the cakes for a few minutes, then loosen the edges, turn out onto a wire rack, and peel off the lining paper. Allow to cool.

4. Make the frosting. Put the butter and half the confectioners' sugar in a mixing bowl, add the dissolved coffee, and beat until smooth. Gradually mix in the remaining confectioners' sugar until pale and creamy.

5. Put one of the cakes on a serving plate, spread with half the frosting, then cover with the second cake. Spread the remaining frosting over the top. Pipe or drizzle swirls of melted chocolate on top.

Eldritch Puddings

Any fan of Lovecraft will know he had a few favorite words and phrases. He loved a "gibbous moon" and a "Cyclopean monolith," but one word that pops up again and again, and has become, for many, synonymous with Lovecraft, is "eldritch." It means "unearthly, weird," which obviously makes it a fitting contestant for his favorite adjective. These puddings are neither unearthly nor weird, but combine two of Lovecraft's other favorite things: chocolate and coffee.

"Down unlit and illimitable corridors of eldritch fantasy sweeps the black, nameless Nemesis that drives me to self-annihilation."

—"The Hound"

Magic happens when you combine coffee and chocolate. Their complex flavors enhance each other perfectly, making them a wonderful combination for these mousses. The ideal make-ahead dessert for entertaining, these look lovely served in little coffee cups and are a light way to end a meal.

SERVES 6

Prep time 20 minutes,
plus chilling

8-ounce bar of bittersweet chocolate

1 tablespoon unsalted butter

3 tablespoons strong black coffee

3 eggs, separated

1. Make chocolate curls by paring the underside of the block of chocolate with a swivel-bladed vegetable peeler. If the curls are very small, microwave the chocolate in 10-second bursts on full power until the chocolate is soft enough to shape. When you have enough curls to decorate six mousses, set aside, then break the remaining chocolate (about 7 ounces) into pieces.

2. Melt the chocolate pieces in a heatproof bowl set over a saucepan of gently simmering water, making sure the bottom of the bowl does not touch the water. Stir the butter into the melted chocolate, then mix in the coffee. Stir in the egg yolks one at a time until the mixture is smooth. Remove the bowl from the pan and let cool.

3. Whisk the egg whites in a clean bowl until soft peaks form, and fold into the chocolate mixture. Pour the mixture into six small coffee cups or ramekin dishes and chill until ready to serve. Serve decorated with the chocolate curls.

Witch-light Truffles

In "The Dreams in the Witch-House," the hapless hero Walter Gilman finds himself inhabiting a room in a boarding house that also seems to be home to the ghostly presence of the witch Keziah Mason, who had fled Salem in 1692. Walter has strange dreams and begins to see a "faint violet glow." A friend warns him that "everybody in Arkham [knows it is] Keziah's witch light, which play[s] near Brown Jenkin [her familiar] and the old crone herself." These decadent dark chocolate truffles are inspired by Keziah's eerie purple glow, and are decorated with beautiful crystallized violets for a witchy finish.

These make a lovely homemade gift—once they are completely set, place the truffles in mini cupcake cases and pack into a gift box lined with pretty tissue paper. For a minty version, add 3–4 tablespoons of mint liqueur to the chocolate truffle mix instead of the brandy or rum.

MAKES 24

Prep time 45 minutes,
plus chilling

1 cup heavy cream
14 ounces bittersweet chocolate
3–4 tablespoons brandy or rum
2 tablespoons cocoa powder, sifted
crystallized violets, to decorate

1. Pour the cream into a small pan and bring to a boil. Take the pan off the heat and break in half the chocolate. Leave to stand until it has melted, then stir in the brandy or rum and mix until smooth. Chill for 4 hours until the truffle mixture is firm.

2. Line a baking sheet with waxed paper and dust with cocoa powder. Scoop a little truffle mixture onto a teaspoon, then transfer it to a second spoon and back to the first again, making a well-rounded egg shape (or use a melon baller). Slide the truffle onto the cocoa-dusted paper. Repeat until all the mixture is used up. Chill again for 2 hours, or overnight if possible, until firm.

3. Melt the remaining chocolate in a bowl over a pan of simmering water, making sure the bottom of the bowl does not touch the water. Stir well, then, holding one truffle at a time on a fork over the bowl, spoon melted chocolate over the top to coat it. Place the truffles on a piece of waxed paper on a nonstick baking sheet. Swirl a little chocolate over the top of each with a spoon and finish with a crystallized violet.

4. Chill for at least 1 hour before serving.

Dunwich Devil's Food Cake

The strange town of Dunwich, the setting for "The Dunwich Horror," has a sinister air. Lovecraft tells us that "outsiders visit Dunwich as seldom as possible," and that the area is full of historic rumors about "witch-blood, Satan-worship and strange forest presences." The story sees what writer John Salonia describes as "a Faustian bargain between the degenerate Old Whateley and the extracosmic entity Yog-Sothoth"—but Lovecraft cleverly updates the idea to make it fit with his own creations. He rejects the ideas of devil worship and witchcraft, telling us "these tales, of course, are obsolete and ridiculous." Instead, as Salonia explains, he "ingeniously subverts all folktales of sorcerers' pacts with devils as superstitious garbled accounts of an ongoing traffic between human beings and the Old Ones." In other words, as an avowed atheist, Lovecraft reframes encounters that may have been superstitiously (and mistakenly) viewed by the locals of Dunwich as meetings with demons or Satan as interactions between humans and the intergalactic beings that dominate his stories. Even if the devil isn't really real, this devil's food cake is darkly delicious, but not (we hope) damning.

Devilishly delicious and decadent, this is a cake that chocolate lovers will want to bake on repeat. Rich, moist cake layered with a luscious sour cream and chocolate ganache frosting, it explodes with chocolatey flavors.

Continued overleaf →

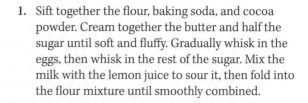

SERVES 12

Prep + cooking time 1 hour,
plus cooling

1¾ cups all-purpose flour
1 teaspoon baking soda
½ cup cocoa powder
9 tablespoons butter
1¼ cups light brown sugar
3 eggs
1 cup milk
1 tablespoon lemon juice

For the frosting
6 ounces bittersweet chocolate
3 ounces milk chocolate
3 tablespoons superfine sugar
1¼ cups sour cream

1. Sift together the flour, baking soda, and cocoa powder. Cream together the butter and half the sugar until soft and fluffy. Gradually whisk in the eggs, then whisk in the rest of the sugar. Mix the milk with the lemon juice to sour it, then fold into the flour mixture until smoothly combined.

2. Grease two 8-inch cake pans, and line the bases with nonstick baking parchment. Spoon the mixture equally into the prepared pans and level over the surface of both.

3. Bake at 350°F for 30 minutes until risen, springy to the touch, and shrinking away from the edges of the pans. Cool in the pans for 10 minutes, then upturn the cakes on to a wire rack to cool.

4. Melt the bittersweet and milk chocolate together in a bowl over a pan of simmering water, making sure the bottom of the bowl does not touch the water, then remove from the heat and whisk in the sugar and sour cream to make the frosting.

5. Slice each cake in half horizontally to make four layers. Put one layer on the serving dish and spread with a fourth of the frosting. Top with another cake layer, then some more frosting. Continue layering cake and frosting, ending with frosting on top.

Under the (Chocolate) Pyramids

Lovecraft occasionally paired up with other writers to create a story together, but one of the more unusual collaborations in his career has to be "Under the Pyramids," the tale of a daring escape from a chamber underneath the pyramids in Egypt that Lovecraft co-wrote with none other than Harry Houdini, the legendary magician and escape artist. The story was based on an experience Houdini claimed to have actually had, although Lovecraft was skeptical and decided to embellish the tale to his own liking, treating it as pure fiction. It's also, interestingly enough, the story that Lovecraft and his new bride Sonia spent their wedding night frantically typing up (see page 15).

This is a take on popular no-bake rocky road, in an elegant pyramid shape. It's super-easy to make—just melt and mix—and you can customize the ingredients: try mini marshmallows, dried cranberries or raspberries, raisins, crushed meringue, Turkish delight, popcorn, or honeycomb. Serve in thin slices, as it is rich.

SERVES 10

Prep + cooking time 30 minutes, plus cooling and setting

10 ounces milk chocolate, broken into pieces

scant ½ cup evaporated milk

16 ounces graham crackers, broken into small pieces

1 cup pitted dates, prunes, or dried apricots, roughly chopped

1 cup mixed nuts, chopped

2 ounces bittersweet chocolate

1. Heat the milk chocolate gently in a heavy pan with the evaporated milk, stirring frequently, until the chocolate has melted. Remove from the heat and transfer to a bowl. Leave until cool, but not set. Stir in the crackers, dried fruits, and nuts.

2. Grease the base and three sides of a 7-inch square cake pan and line with plastic wrap. Prop up one side of the pan so that it sits at an angle of 45 degrees and the unlined side of the pan is uppermost. Spoon in the cake mixture and level the surface. Leave until firm, then transfer to the refrigerator to set completely. Remove the cake from the pan and peel away the plastic wrap.

3. To melt the bittersweet chocolate, break into chunks into a heatproof bowl over a pan of gently simmering water, making sure the base of the bowl does not touch the water. Don't stir until it looks melted, then stir a couple of times until smooth.

4. Using a teaspoon, drizzle lines of melted chocolate over the cake. Leave to set again, then serve thinly sliced.

Grandpa Theobold's Ice Cream Sundae

Lovecraft adored ice cream, and often mentioned it in his letters. He sometimes ate ice cream in lieu of a meal (including at breakfast—see page 24), and in 1927 he even enjoyed an ice-cream-eating contest with some of his Kalem Club friends, sampling twenty-eight different flavors. Although he only lived to be forty-six, Lovecraft was an old man at heart, and sometimes jokingly referred to himself as "Grandpa" or "Grandpa Theobold," so we decided to name this delightful ice cream sundae after his grandfatherly alter ego.

Prepped in a flash, this sweet treat for the whole family makes great use of store-bought ingredients. For adults use kirsch, or go for cherry syrup for an alcohol-free version. You can use ready-made chocolate sauce or, if you have a little extra time, try the homemade Maple-Chocolate Sauce on page 98.

SERVES 4

Prep time 10 minutes

3 cups cherries, halved and pitted

¼ cup kirsch or cherry syrup

16 ounces vanilla ice cream

2 double chocolate muffins, coarsely chopped

½ cup store-bought chocolate sauce

1¼ cups heavy whipping cream

To serve

4 cherries on their stems

a little grated chocolate

1. Place a few of the cherries in the bottom of four tall sundae glasses and spoon 1 tablespoon of the kirsch or cherry syrup into each glass. Add two small scoops of vanilla ice cream to each glass. Divide half the muffin pieces among the glasses and spoon 1 tablespoon chocolate sauce over each.

2. Repeat with another layer of cherries, ice cream, muffins, and chocolate sauce, finishing with an extra layer of cherries.

3. Lightly whip the cream in a bowl with a handheld electric mixer until soft peaks form and spoon over the sundaes. Decorate with the cherries on their stems and a little grated chocolate. Serve immediately with long spoons.

H.P.'s Coffee Ice Cream

Another ice cream recipe, because Lovecraft really did adore the stuff. In a 1925 letter to his aunt, he declared, "Ice cream I dote upon," reminding her a few months later that it was "a substance of which I never become wearied." In other letters, he complains that it is impossible to get coffee-flavored ice cream in New York; it was, apparently, "a wholly Novanglian institution." We hope this light and fluffy zabaglione with espresso sauce would meet his standards.

This is a boozy, special-occasion dessert for the adults, laced with both sweet Marsala and coffee liqueur. It has a soft and creamy texture because it isn't churned and is wonderful here with darkly rich and syrupy coffee sauce spooned over.

SERVES 6

Prep + cooking time 25 minutes, plus freezing

6 egg yolks
½ cup superfine sugar
6 tablespoons sweet Marsala
1¼ cups heavy cream
30 ladyfingers

For the coffee sauce
¾ cup cold espresso coffee
½ cup granulated sugar
3 tablespoons coffee-flavored liqueur

1. Beat the egg yolks with the superfine sugar in a heatproof bowl set over a saucepan of gently simmering water until the sugar has melted. Add the Marsala and continue beating for another 6–8 minutes, or until the mixture has thickened and holds its shape.

2. Whip the cream in a bowl until soft peaks form. Gently fold in the egg mixture. Roughly break the ladyfingers, then fold into the egg mixture. Tip into a 4½ x 8½-inch loaf pan lined with plastic wrap. Cover with plastic wrap and freeze for at least 6 hours or overnight until set.

3. Make the coffee sauce. Heat the coffee in a small saucepan, add the granulated sugar, and stir until melted. Add the liqueur and boil vigorously until the sauce becomes thick and syrupy.

4. Turn the ice cream out onto a serving plate and spoon over the sauce, which can be warm or at room temperature. Serve cut into slices.

H. P. Lovecraft as a Host

The members of the Kalem Club took it in turns to host their gatherings, providing their guests with food and drink to fuel their sometimes night-long sessions. When it was his turn to host, Lovecraft took his duties very seriously. As we saw on page 119, he bought an aluminum pail, which he used to fetch fresh, hot coffee for his friends, and he also took pains to ensure he had provided their favorite treats and presented them in a pleasing manner.

In one letter to his Aunt Lillian, he writes: "At 11pm, I served the refreshments, getting out tip-table, Japanese trays, blue china, 454 Spoons, R.A.P. forks & triangularly folded paper napkins. Using my new aluminum pail, I went out for some excellent coffee; & all hands pronounced the lunch a marked success both as a social event & dietary incident."

The "454 Spoons" he refers to here are spoons from his childhood home at 454 Angell Street in Providence, a grand and richly furnished house that he and his mother were forced to leave after his grandfather's death. "R.A.P." must refer to his maternal grandmother, Robie Alzada Place Phillips, suggesting that even in his impoverished circumstances, Lovecraft still held on to a few precious pieces of his family's more salubrious past—even if they were only spoons and forks.

On days when he was reluctant to have company in New York, Lovecraft would hide himself away in an alcove in his apartment, taking care not to let any light shine out from his windows or beneath his door, so that any callers would think he was out. His friend George Kirk lived upstairs, however, and would sometimes tap on the radiator pipe to see if Lovecraft was in. On one such evening, Kirk made his usual taps, and confessed to his friend that he was hungry, but didn't feel like dressing to go out to eat. Lovecraft told his aunt: "Now I too was about to dine, so with the utmost hospitality I invited him down, treated him to A & P spaghetti, cheese, bread, and vanilla wafers off my best blue china, and bade him a courtly adieu almost immediately afterward."

If you do feel like company, here are some tips for hosting a literary salon or dinner party, Lovecraft style:

- Use your best blue china, and if you have any family heirlooms in the form of cutlery, place them on the table to share with your guests.

- Always supply fresh coffee—ideally sourced from a local coffee shop and transported in an aluminum pail.

- Make use of ambient lighting—Lovecraft favored "a candle-lit table pleasantly suggesting my eighteenth century."

- And—most importantly—always fold your napkins into triangles.

"So revel and chaff as ye thirstily quaff: under six feet of dirt 'tis less easy to laugh!"

—*Jervas Dudley's song, "The Tomb"*

Potions &
Concoctions

Lovecraft was a lifelong teetotaler, favoring ginger beer, orangeade, and his beloved coffee over alcoholic concoctions; in fact, on the same occasion that he and his friends cooked up their own chili (see page 62), Lovecraft was bemused when one of his companions brought along a six-pack of beer, asking, "What are you going to do with so much of it?"

Despite this, his work is so full of mystical drinks, "violently bubbling cauldron[s]" ("The Alchemist") and shimmering liquids in "fantastic flasks, crucibles, alembics, and furnaces" (*The Case of Charles Dexter Ward*) that we couldn't resist creating a few cocktails. If you need a little Dutch courage to see you through some of Lovecraft's scarier stories, try a hit of a Necronomicon Negroni (page 144) or a taste of Barzai's Moonshine (page 140) to steady your nerves. The Alchemist's Elixir (page 146) might not give you eternal life, but it will certainly take the edge off.

For those, like Lovecraft, who prefer to take their scares sober, try the Gibbous Moon (page 152), a zingy fresh lemonade, or the Juice of Deeper Slumber (page 154) to help you drift off into the dream-lands.

"Here—have another drink—I need one anyhow!"

—*"Pickman's Model"*

Rhode Island Iced Tea

Lovecraft was born in Rhode Island and spent much of his life in the state, apart from the few years he lived in New York. He spent much of his time in the Big Apple longing to return to his native Providence (see page 12), so we've renamed this classic drink in honor of his beloved New England home, where so much of his weird fiction was set—and where he created his own periodical, the *Rhode Island Journal of Astronomy*, in 1903, when he would have been just twelve or thirteen.

Featuring Cointreau, a French orange-flavored liqueur, and topped up with plenty of ice and cola, this is a long drink but a strong one, so savor it. Use freshly squeezed lemon juice if possible because it makes all the difference to the taste. You'll need a cocktail shaker, strainer, and two highball glasses.

MAKES 2

Prep time 5 minutes

1 measure vodka
1 measure gin
1 measure white rum
1 measure tequila
1 measure Cointreau
1 measure lemon juice
ice cubes
cola, to top up
lemon slices, to decorate

1. Put the vodka, gin, rum, tequila, Cointreau, and lemon juice in a cocktail shaker with some ice cubes and shake to mix.

2. Strain into two highball glasses filled with ice cubes and top up with cola. Decorate with lemon slices and serve.

The Outsider's Nepenthe

T he Outsider" is among the most traditionally gothic of Lovecraft's works, and is believed by many to be autobiographical, depicting as it does a narrator who is cut off from the rest of society, which could perhaps reflect the author's own reclusive teenage years. Lovecraft scholar S. T. Joshi describes the story as "heavily Poe-inspired," and it's easy to see why: it is set in a strange, dark castle that is "infinitely old and infinitely horrible; full of dark passages and having high ceilings where the eye could find only cobwebs and shadows." Lovecraft himself admitted in a 1931 letter to J. Vernon Shea that the work "represents my literal though unconscious imitation of Poe at its very height." The tale sees the Outsider making a discovery so horrific that he turns to nepenthe, a potion used in Greek mythology to overcome sadness by inducing forgetfulness. So be careful how many of these you have . . .

Get out your cocktail shaker and shake, rattle, and pour for this zingy recipe. Freshly squeezed lemon juice—and it really must be freshly squeezed for this one—lifts the spicy, fruity notes of Southern Comfort.

Continued overleaf →

SERVES 2

Prep time 5 minutes

crushed ice
4 measures Southern Comfort
2 measures lemon juice
1 measure maple syrup
chilled champagne, to top up
lemon zest strips, to decorate

1. Put 8–10 crushed ice cubes in a cocktail shaker. Pour the Southern Comfort, lemon juice, and maple syrup over the ice and shake until a frost forms on the outside of the shaker.

2. Strain into two champagne flutes and top up with chilled champagne. Decorate with a lemon zest strip and serve.

"But in the cosmos there is balm as
well as bitterness, and that
balm is nepenthe."

Barzai's Moonshine

"The Other Gods," described by S. T. Joshi and David E. Schultz as "a textbook example of hubris," is a tale that clearly echoes Lovecraft's admiration for the Irish fantasy writer Lord Dunsany, whose influence can be seen in the style, content, and naming conventions in many of his works. In fact, in a 1923 letter to Clark Ashton Smith, Lovecraft remarked that "Dunsany has influenced me more than anyone else except Poe." "The Other Gods" sees an elderly scholar named Barzai the Wise decide to climb the "high and rocky Hatheg-Kla" in an effort to set eyes on the earth gods, who have increasingly moved away from the world of men. The gods are said to come on a moonlit night when clouds will hide their meeting place on the summit from the mortals below—but what Barzai discovers when he reaches the mountaintop is something else entirely.

A vibrant shade of blue, evocative of the glorious blue of tropical seas and skies, this elegant cocktail owes its color to blue Curaçao. An aromatic orange-flavored liqueur, Curaçao gets its taste from the dried peel of the laraha, a citrus tree grown on the Caribbean island of Curaçao.

SERVES 2

Prep time 5 minutes

ice cubes
4 measures gin
1 measure blue Curaçao
red or blue cocktail cherries, to decorate

1. Put eight ice cubes into a cocktail shaker. Pour in the gin and blue Curaçao. Shake well to mix.

2. Strain into two martini glasses and carefully drop a cherry into each glass.

Moon-tree Wine

In *The Dream-Quest of Unknown Kadath*, while he is with the zoogs (who, incidentally, inspired the recipe on page 88), our hero Carter is given a drink: "a gourd of fermented sap from a haunted tree unlike the others, which had grown from a seed dropt down by someone on the moon." Carter later uses this mysterious "moon-tree wine" to trick the patriarch Atal into becoming "irresponsibly talkative" and revealing his secrets. So make sure you enjoy this particular tipple only with people you trust, or you could end up revealing secrets of your own.

When balmy summer evenings call for gathering outside with friends and enjoying something chilled, this cooler is the perfect crowd-pleaser to serve. Peach schnapps and fresh peaches give it a fragrant fruity note. Elderflower cordial is available online and from specialty stores.

SERVES 6–8

Prep time 5 minutes

25-ounce bottle dry white wine, chilled
scant ½ cup elderflower cordial
¾ cup peach schnapps
4 cups soda water, chilled
3 peaches, pitted and sliced
ice cubes

1. Place all the ingredients in a pitcher and mix gently.

Necronomicon Negroni

*T*he *Necronomicon* is a mythical book of the occult. It was created by Lovecraft and appears in many of his stories, but it has taken on a life of its own, with some people believing that the book actually exists, and even producing their own versions of it. Lovecraft named its supposed author Abdul Alhazred, a name he said was suggested to him by a family friend when he was a young boy. *The Necronomicon* includes such dark wisdom as: "Nor is it to be thought . . . that man is either the oldest of earth's masters, or that the common bulk of life and substance walks alone. The Old Ones were, the Old Ones are, and the Old Ones shall be" ("The Dunwich Horror"). The sinister book is referenced in many of Lovecraft's works, including *At the Mountains of Madness* and "The Call of Cthulhu," and has become an integral part of the Cthulhu Mythos.

Enjoy this delicious negroni, and raise a glass to one of the most famous books that never was.

Refreshingly bitter and herby, this Italian cocktail is all about balance so includes equal measures of gin, vermouth, and Campari. You'll need a couple of old-fashioned glasses to serve it in, plus a mixing glass, long-handled spoon, and a strainer to make it.

SERVES 2

Prep time 5 minutes

ice cubes

2 measures Plymouth gin

2 measures Campari

2 measures red vermouth

soda water, to top up (optional)

orange wedges, to decorate

1. Put some ice cubes into a mixing glass and fill two old-fashioned glasses with ice cubes.

2. Add the gin, Campari, and vermouth to the mixing glass, stir briefly to mix, and strain over the ice in the glasses. Top up with soda water, if desired. Decorate each glass with some orange wedges and serve.

Floating Brain

The strange, crablike extraterrestrial creatures of "The Whisperer in Darkness" are said to have come to Earth in search of a particular metal, but also "men of learning," whom they carry away with them to their home planet. Apparently, the human body cannot make the "cosmic voyage" across the "interstellar void"—but the human brain can. So, we are told, "the Outer Ones had found a way to convey human brains without their concomitant physical structure," extracting them from the body and transporting them in a neat metal canister full of special fluid. This is thought to be one of the earliest examples of the idea of a surviving isolated brain, although the disembodied head or brain has since become a regular trope in science fiction, from the 1962 film *The Brain That Wouldn't Die* and the cymeks in *The Legends of Dune* to the numerous talking heads in *Futurama*.

This fun and slightly gruesome shot creates the illusion of a brain bobbing around in one of the Outer Ones' transportation devices.

Chill two shot glasses in the fridge or freezer before you make this cocktail. You need a bar spoon, or long-handled spoon, plus a steady hand for pouring. Going slow and gentle is the trick here.

SERVES 2

Prep time 5 minutes

2 measures peach schnapps
2 dashes Baileys Irish Cream
6 drops grenadine

1. Pour the schnapps into two chilled shot glasses.

2. Using the back of a bar spoon, slowly float the Baileys over the schnapps. Very gently, drop the grenadine on top of the Baileys; it will gradually ease through this top layer and fall to the bottom of the glass.

The Alchemist's Elixir

"The Alchemist" is one of Lovecraft's earliest offerings, first published in the *United Amateur* in 1916. It tells the story of Antoine, "last of the unhappy and accursed Comtes de C——," who lives in the "vast and gloomy chambers" of a crumbling château. Antoine reveals that back in the thirteenth century, an alchemist named Michel Mauvais had lived on the family's once-grand estate, and that he spent his days "seeking such things as the Philosopher's Stone, or the Elixir of Eternal Life." Mauvais was murdered by Antoine's ancestor, and the alchemist's son, Charles le Sorcier, swore revenge. He cursed the rich family, splashing "a phial of colorless liquid" in the Comte's face. Ever since, every Comte has died at the age of thirty-two, a milestone that Antoine is fast approaching. This delightful tipple is our tribute to "the elixir which should grant to him who partook of it eternal life and youth."

Cool, bright mint and rich chocolate are a time-honored pairing, as featured in this cocktail, with its distinctive white and bright green layers. Like an after-dinner mint in a glass, it's ideal to round off a meal instead of dessert.

SERVES 2

Prep time 5 minutes

2 measures crème de cacao
2 measures crème de menthe
mint sprigs, to decorate

1. Pour the crème de cacao into two martini glasses.

2. Using the back of a bar spoon, float the crème de menthe over the crème de cacao to create a separate layer. Decorate with mint sprigs and serve.

Reanimator

Herbert West—Reanimator" may be one of Lovecraft's better-known stories, thanks in part to the cult 1980s film loosely based on it, Stuart Gordon's *Re-Animator*. Lovecraft's original version is narrated by a medical student who tells us about his friend Herbert West, who "had already made himself notorious through his wild theories on the nature of death and the possibility of overcoming it artificially." After experimenting on various animals with mixed results, West becomes fixated on the idea of carrying out the procedure on a human corpse—preferably one as fresh as possible.

We've all had those days when we feel like death; this espresso-spiked mocktail will perk you up more effectively than West's strange serum. We think the coffee-loving teetotaler Lovecraft would have been thrilled with this concoction.

This is a chilled take on the much-loved Irish coffee. Served with delicious almondy cookies alongside, it's a refreshingly sweet and creamy way to finish off a meal. For an extra kick, you could add a shot of Irish whiskey too.

Continued overleaf →

SERVES 4

Prep + cook time 20 minutes

For the almond cookies

1¾ cups ground almonds (almond meal)

1 cup granulated sugar

½ teaspoon baking powder

1 egg white, lightly beaten

confectioners' sugar, for dusting

For the cocktail

½ cup strong coffee, cooled

¼ cup coffee liqueur

¼–⅓ cup heavy cream

1. Line a baking sheet with baking parchment. Put the almonds, sugar, and baking powder in a bowl and stir through the beaten egg white to make a soft paste. Knead briefly, then roll into a long cylinder. Slice off ½-inch pieces and lightly pinch each end to make oval shapes. Place on the baking sheet and bake at 400°F for 10 minutes, or until pale golden. Let cool and dust with plenty of confectioners' sugar.

2. Meanwhile, make the cocktail. Mix together the coffee and coffee liqueur and pour into four martini glasses. Slowly pour in the cream over the back of a teaspoon so it settles on the top. Serve with the cookies.

Shoggoth Shot

In *At the Mountains of Madness*, we learn that shoggoths are vast, alarming creatures originally bred by the Elder Things as slaves to build their cities. The narrator, Dyer, tells us gravely that "shoggoths and their work ought not to be seen by human beings or portrayed by any beings"—although he then suffers the misfortune of seeing one for himself. These shapeless monsters, formed of "viscous agglutinations of bubbling cells," are genuinely terrifying, so soothe your nerves with these shots, where the passion fruit pulp echoes the shoggoths' weird, bloblike form.

The orange flavor of Triple Sec is complemented by the tartness of passion fruit pulp in these shots. You'll need to remember to pop the shot glasses into the freezer for a few minutes beforehand as they should be chilled for serving.

SERVES 2

Prep time 5 minutes

ice cubes

2 measures silver tequila

2 dashes Triple Sec

2 dashes lime juice

2 passion fruit

1. Put some ice cubes in a cocktail shaker, add the tequila, Triple Sec, and lime juice, and shake well.

2. Strain into two chilled shot glasses. Cut the passion fruit in half and squeeze the pulp over the shots before serving.

"It was a terrible, indescribable thing vaster than any subway train—a shapeless congeries of protoplasmic bubbles, faintly self-luminous, and with myriads of temporary eyes forming and unforming as pustules of greenish light . . ."

The Gibbous Moon

As an avid astronomer from an early age, Lovecraft adored the night sky, and the moon is a recurring theme in his fiction: sometimes full, sometimes barely a sliver, but one of his favorite descriptors for it seems to be "gibbous." A gibbous moon is one that is somewhere between a full moon and a half-moon, and this, it seems, offers the best light for sinister happenings.

This delicious lemonade is as crisp and refreshing as a sliver of moonlight, while the roundness of the lemons lends it a lunar feel.

> "It is at night, when the moon is gibbous and waning, that I see the thing."
>
> —*"Dagon"*

For fresh limeade, follow the recipe below and simply use six limes in place of the four lemons, or you could use a mixture of the two. Try adding chopped mint while the limeade cools for a refreshing mint zing.

SERVES 6-8

Prep + cooking time 10 minutes, plus cooling

⅓ cup superfine sugar

7½ cups water

4 lemons, sliced, plus extra slices to decorate

ice cubes

1. Place the sugar in a pan with 2½ cups of the measured water and all the sliced lemons. Bring to a boil, stirring well until all the sugar has dissolved.

2. Remove from the heat and add all the remaining water. Stir, then set aside to cool completely.

3. Once cold, roughly crush the lemons to release all the juice. Strain through a strainer, add the ice cubes, and serve in glasses decorated with slices of lemon.

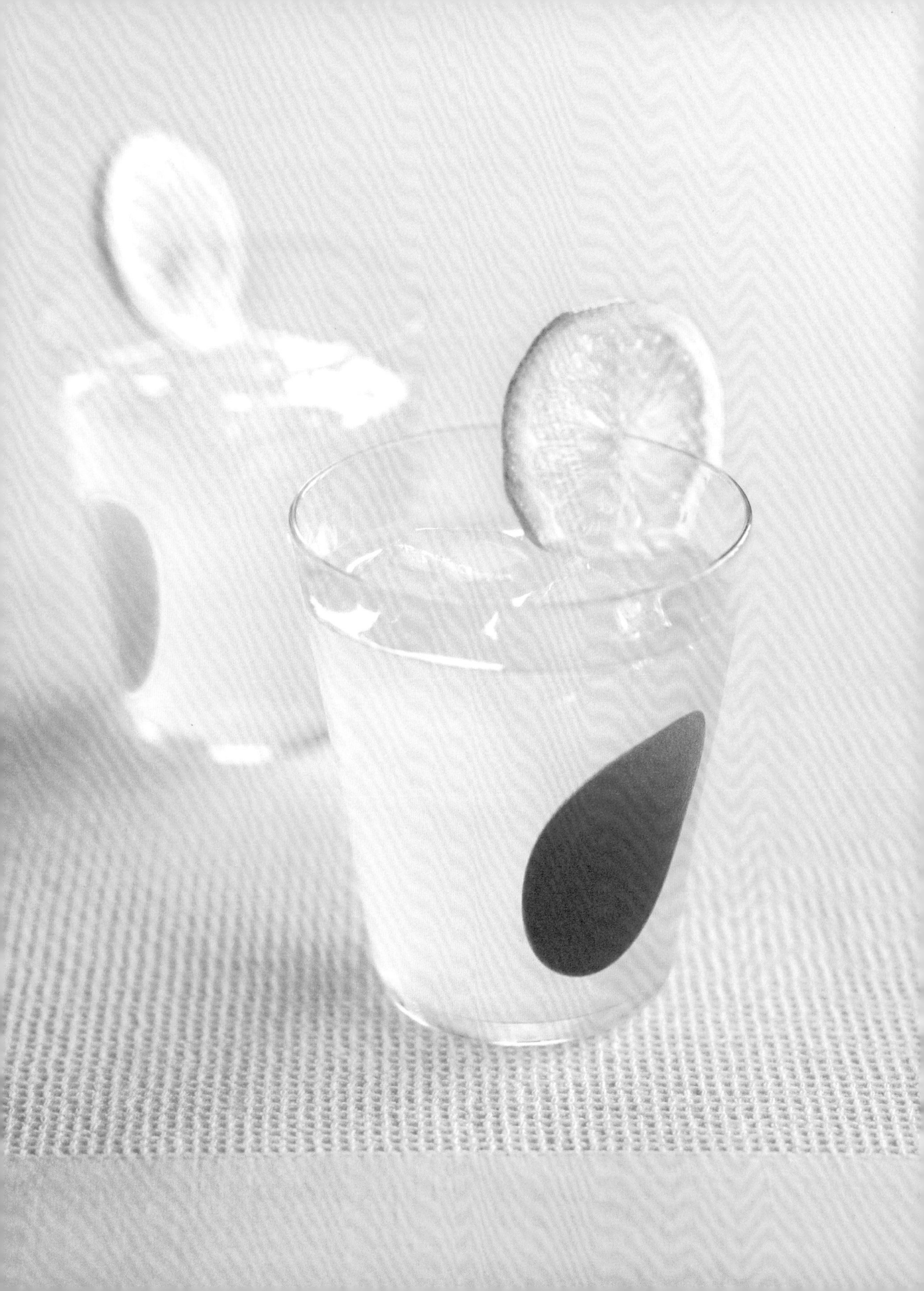

The Juice of Deeper Slumber

At the start of his many adventures in *The Dream-Quest of Unknown Kadath*, the hero Carter must go deep into the dream-lands, and so we are told: "he boldly descended the seven hundred steps to the Gate of Deeper Slumber and set out through the enchanted wood." If seven hundred steps sounds like a few too many, this juice, packed with soporific lettuce and soothing camomile, might help you reach your own dream-lands a little more easily.

The ancient Greeks and Romans believed that lettuce helped induce sleep, and camomile tea is a common go-to for its soporific effect. So when sleep is elusive, try this juice, which combines the delicate floral flavor of camomile tea with lemon and lettuce.

SERVES 1

Prep time 5 minutes

1½ cups lettuce, leaves torn or roughly chopped

½ lemon, peeled

½ cup chilled camomile tea

ice cubes

1. Juice the lettuce and lemon using a juicer or blender until smooth.

2. Mix with the chilled camomile tea until well combined. Serve in a glass over ice.

Cosmic Horror

"The oldest and strongest emotion of mankind is fear, and the oldest and strongest kind of fear is fear of the unknown."

—*H. P. Lovecraft*, Supernatural Horror in Literature

There aren't many writers out there who can claim to have had such influence—and such a unique style—that their name has been transformed into an adjective. Dickens is one; Orwell is another. And so is H. P. Lovecraft. But what does "Lovecraftian" mean?

It goes beyond writing that echoes Lovecraft's own occasionally grandiloquent prose and his fondness for unusual adjectives; if a piece of writing—or an idea—is considered Lovecraftian, it means it instills in us a sense of horror that is more than disgust or shock. Instead, it is a kind of dizzying, soaring fear of the unknowable: an awareness of the vastness and indifference of the universe, the unseen things it may contain, and our own insignificance within it. It is a terror of, to use his own words, "the hidden and fathomless worlds of strange life which may pulsate in the gulfs beyond the stars" (*Supernatural Horror in Literature*). It is a creeping sense of dread, preoccupied with the far reaches of the cosmos and the hidden depths of the oceans or subterranean lairs—and the dawning knowledge that nobody is coming to save you.

One of the remarkable things about Lovecraft's work is how often these supernatural terrors are presented against a backdrop of apparent mundanity. Some of his tales do take place in ancient Antarctic cities (*At the Mountains of Madness*) or mystical dream-lands (*The Dream-Quest of Unknown Kadath*), but often the horror comes from the sense of uncanniness and wrongness found in the juxtaposition of a cosmic deity or extraterrestrial creature with sleepy New England towns: much of the dread in "The Shadow over Innsmouth," for example, comes from the fact that the narrator is able to hop on a bus and take a day trip to this cursed place while on a merry sightseeing tour of the local area. Throughout Lovecraft's work, the ordinary—a cup of coffee, a bowl of soup, an apple orchard, or a suburban house—is overcome by the extraordinary: the coffee is poisoned by an alien being; the soup is served by a man who bears a queasy resemblance to a fish or toad; the apple orchard is struck by a meteor that renders the fruit inedible; the suburban house is overgrown by a sinister, shadowy fungus, or hides a portal to another dimension.

Lovecraft's interest in science and astronomy can be seen throughout his work; he was a voracious reader, and his biographer S. T. Joshi notes that "in later years, Lovecraft professed to an acute, persistent, unquenchable craving to *know*." And yet, in his works, it is often this desire to know that damns his characters. Too much knowledge is forbidden; many of his narrators are driven mad by what they see or discover. This is perhaps best exemplified by the fictitious *Necronomicon*, a book of occult lore that appears in many of Lovecraft's stories; when it is read, something terrible usually happens.

Lovecraftian or cosmic horror continues to have an influence on writers and creators today. Authors including Stephen King, Alan Moore, and Ramsey Campbell have cited Lovecraft as an influence, while filmmakers such as John Carpenter and Guillermo del Toro have taken inspiration from his works and ideas. Although Lovecraft never saw success in his own lifetime, it is fitting that his cosmic creations and extraterrestrial horrors have lived on and become timeless.

Index

References

An H. P. Lovecraft Encyclopedia, S. T. Joshi and David E. Schultz, Greenwood Press, 2001.
H. P. Lovecraft: Letters to Family & Friends—Volume 1, edited by S. T. Joshi and David E. Schultz, Hippocampus Press, 2020.
H. P. Lovecraft: Letters to Family & Friends—Volume 2, edited by S. T. Joshi and David E. Schultz, Hippocampus Press, 2020.
H. P. Lovecraft: A Short Biography, S. T. Joshi, Sarnath Press, 2018.
The Complete Tales of H. P. Lovecraft, Quarto, 2019.
The Poetry of H. P. Lovecraft, Ragged Hand, 2020.
H. P. Lovecraft: Selected Letters, Vol. 5—1934–1937, edited by *August Derleth and James Turner*, Arkham House Publishers, 1976.
Supernatural Horror in Literature, H. P. Lovecraft, Dover Publications, 1973.

Picture Acknowledgements

Illustration: Mauro Mazzara 6, 9, 10, 16, 21, 22, 27, 28, 35, 36, 40, 45, 51, 58, 64, 69, 78, 83, 89, 96, 121, 124, 134, 138, 147, 150

Photography: Octopus Publishing Group

Cover illustrations: Yoko Obata/iStock, inspiring/Shutterstock